Academic Language & Academic Vocabulary

A K-12 Guide to Content Learning

& Response to Intervention (RTI)

D1319350

Eli R. Johnson

Achievement For All Publishers
Sacramento, CA 95682
(530) 391-1249
www.achievement4all.org

For information about permission to reproduce selections from this book please call (530) 391-1249

Author: Johnson, Eli R.

Title: Academic Language & Academic Vocabulary: RTI Strategies for content learning

ISBN: 0615576230

ISBN 13: 9780615576237

Table of Contents

About the Author

Eli Johnson has worked as a Classroom Teacher, School Principal, Director of Curriculum & Instruction, and Assistant Superintendent of Instruction. He has served as a consultant to the California Department of Education supporting early literacy ($100 Million Program), English language professional development ($56 Million Program), and math/science partnerships ($34 Million Program). He earned his teaching degree from Brigham Young University and a master's degree in education leadership from the University of Washington. In 2010, Eli led an elementary school to the highest annual percentage gain (+140) of any of the 10,000 schools in the state of California. He also directed a high school with 90% English Language Learners to become the recipient of the U.S. News and World Report Medal Award Honors. In 2009 every school under Eli's direction achieved double digit gains on the annual statewide assessments.

As a nationally recognized speaker and consultant, Eli works with teachers and leaders to address the fundamental issues behind the achievement gap. He also works with schools to support adolescent literacy, school leadership, and other issues affecting student achievement. Eli has worked for both public and non-profit educational organizations to create sustainable educational reform.

You can contact Eli by e-mail at eli@achievement4all.org.

Acknowledgements

This book is dedicated to my mother who was my first and most inspiring teacher. And, a big thank you goes out to all of the dedicated teachers who inspire students every day.

Other Books by Eli Johnson

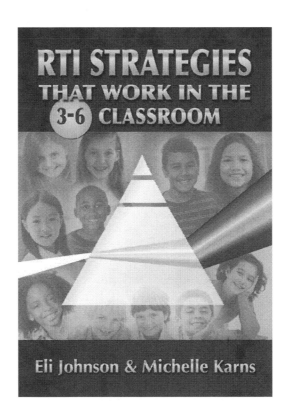

Chapter One:
Academic Interventions
For our Schools

*"It is the supreme art of the teacher
to awaken joy in creative
expression and knowledge."*

Albert Einstein

Natalie struggled to focus on the page in front of her. The teacher had been writing things on the board and explaining the lesson, but her mind seemed to wander off and think about what was happening outside on the bright spring morning. They said she had a learning disability, whatever that means. All she knew is that concentrating for very long was almost impossible. When she was in Kindergarten she couldn't even read the board from the back of the classroom, but she didn't get called on very often so maybe no one noticed she really didn't know what she was supposed to be learning. Because the board was blurry, paying attention to other things soon became an engrained habit. It seemed she faked her way through first grade too. It wasn't until second grade at a vision check-up from a doctor that the school finally realized she needed glasses. She got glasses and that helped her see the board which was terrific, but her ability to concentrate for longer than 15 minutes was extremely difficult. Her third grade teacher also noticed concerned and she went through a bunch of testing. They said that she had a learning disability—something called Attention Deficit Disorder or ADD. The fact that she was a sweet, quiet girl had helped hide from others her inability to focus and concentrate on the learning at hand. She went to doctors who gave her exercises for visually tracking and reading, yet it seemed that when she would read her eyes just bounced around the page. She was behind her peers, yet her teachers didn't really know what to with her. School was a struggle and it felt like it always would be—unless she received some help.

Introduction

Within education comes plenty of sticky students who bring with them many different challenges to their learning. In fact, American education is at a crossroads. It seems that we have been here for quite some time. Many of our students do very well in school while other students always seem to struggle in school. The following statistics show the alarming rate of students that are dropping out of our schools and the high percentage of minority students that are most affected:

- *Every school year 1.2 million of our youth drop out of high school (Alliance for Education, 2006). The most commonly cited reason is the lack of literacy skills to negotiate the demands of school (Kamil, 2003; Snow & Biancarosa, 2003).*

- *Over 40% of African-American students and 45% of Hispanic students fail to graduate from high school with their peers (Orfield, Losen, Wald, & Swanson, 2004).*

- *The overall rate in America of students that fail to graduate on time is 28.3% (Edweek, 2011).*

- *More than 75% of school drop-outs mentioned difficulties in their literacy ability to read in core content classes significantly contributed to their decision to drop out (Lyon, 2001).*

The end result is that our schools are reinforcing a dynamic of academic haves and academic have-nots. Some students are doing extremely well while others are struggling mightily. Steve McClung, President of McGraw-Hill share the this staggering information,

"More than 3,000 students drop out of high school every day, and the most commonly cited reason is the lack of literacy skills. A staggering 40 percent of all middle and high school students cannot even read at a basic literacy level according to Reading Next."

The literacy rates in third world countries have been steadily increasing over the past several decades. The gap between educated countries that can compete in the world and those that have lacked the intellectual capital in years past is diminishing rapidly. The increased literacy ability of these countries, particularly in math and science, has leveled that economic playing field. Students who graduate from school now are truly competing in a global economy. In a world that is connected by the world-wide-web, the ability to be literate and communicate formally and effectively is an extremely valuable commodity. Literacy is the ability to listen and think, speak, read, and write effectively. Education has been key in helping so many countries bridge the gap between the economic haves and have nots in the world. At the same time in our own country a gap seems to be widening between those that achieve academically and those that struggle and drop out. At a time when human intellectual capital is at a premium, our nation is seeing increasing drop-out rates. Our school systems are struggling when we compare our results to other first-world countries. As a nation, we are average in reading and science and very much below average in mathematics compared to other first-world countries.

- *The Programme for International Student Assessment (PISA) report, which compares the knowledge and skills of 15-year-olds in countries around the world, ranked the United States out of 34 first world (OECD) countries for 14th reading skills, 17th for science and a below-average 25th for mathematics (2010).*

Where we remain number one in the world is in our advanced education. More and more students are coming from other countries to America to attend the best universities in the world. So the good news is that as a nation our collegiate education system should continue to keep our nation near the top. Yet, only about 20% of our high school seniors go on to four-year colleges, while at the same time we have approximately 14% of adults that remain functionally illiterate. Being functionally illiterate affects the quality of people's lives in a myriad of ways. The simplest evidence is how literacy rates affect our prison system.

- *85% of the youth who appear before the juvenile courts are functionally illiterate (Kozol, 1995).*
- *63% of adult prisoners are functionally illiterate. (Britt, 2009)*

The point of all this data is to recognize that there is a huge gulf between the academic haves and have-nots and this contributes to the economic haves and have-nots that exist in America. We have some students that are able to access the best universities in the world, while other students struggle to read the front-page of the local newspaper. Bill Gates (TED Conference, 2009) notes that,

"If you are low income in the United States you have a better chance of going to jail than you do of getting a four year degree."

So we have a gap in achievement and a gap in opportunity in the United States. And, this gap dramatically affects individual students and it greatly affects the future health of our nation.

Outcomes of Book

This book will address several key issues in education. Understanding these fundamental issues will improve our classrooms, our school, and the education we provide to the next generation. The following topics will be addressed by looking at what the research says about improving our schools for the future.

- **Achievement Gap**
- **RTI Framework**
- **Classroom Solutions**
- **Academic Language Strategies**
- **Academic Literacy Strategies**
- **Learning Intervention Strategies**
- **Systemic Solutions**

As we gain a deeper understanding of the educational outcomes we will be more prepared to meet the many challenges our students bring to school each day.

Achievement Gap

Why is there an achievement gap? Most every American is aware that there is an achievement gap between students in America. The most obvious gap is between those who are poor and those who socio-economically advantaged. Yet, the basis for the achievement gap and how it affects poor students is cause for concern. The achievement gap profoundly affects millions of students that attend school every day. The children who are most affected by the achievement gap are those that are often the most marginalized (Honig, Diamond, & Gutlohn, 2001).

Children Most Affected by the Achievement Gap

1. *Children Raised in Poverty*

2. *Children who are English language learners*

3. *Children who struggle with reading, phonological processing, memory difficulties, speech or hearing impairments*

We need to focus our energy and our efforts on these students to make sure that we can minimize the effects of the achievement gap. As we provide interventions for our neediest students the results can be amazing. This book will address the roots of the achievement gap and offer *specific step-by-step classroom strategies for addressing the achievement gap*, while also looking at the larger systemic issues that can provide solutions to the achievement gap.

We need an Intervention

Our schools and specifically our students need targeted interventions that will help address the academic issues that are causing an alarming drop-out rate and high rates of illiteracy. The need for interventions has been outlined by the U.S. Department of Education in what they call Response to Intervention or (RTI) its more common acronym. An RTI approach to addressing the gaps in learning that affect achievement has created quite a few changes to how instruction is provided to students. RTI looks to redirect students from a path of academic failure to a path of academic self-sufficiency. Let's begin by looking at definitions of *response and intervention* from Dictionary.com (2010):

Response   1. *An answer or reply to a situation.*
                2. *A chosen course of action that addresses a specific issue.*

Intervention 1. *An interference that re-directs the current path an individual is on.*
                2. *Actions that produce a positive change in results and outcomes.*

The RTI process typically follows a Three-Tier (Tier I, Tier II, & Tier III) model that begins with a focus on interventions in the classroom (Bernhardt & Hebert, 2011).

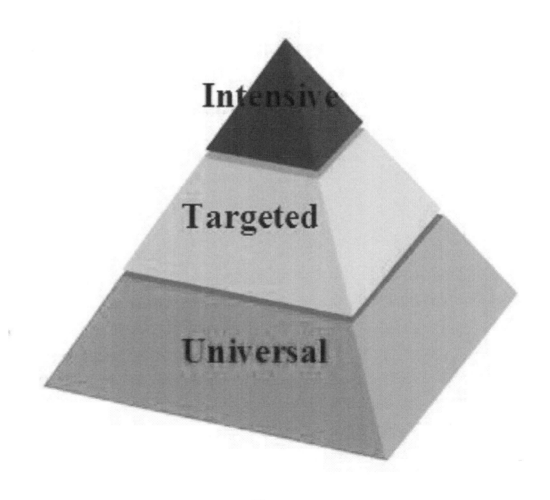

The most important of the three levels is Tier I, because quality first instruction with sufficient support can keep most students from falling behind.

Three Tiered RTI Framework

Tier 1 -   Classroom Interventions benefit all students and they should effectively reach 80% of students.   These interventions are designed to be proactively delivered to prevent students from falling behind.   These strategies are typically delivered through whole-group or small-group instruction.

Tier 2 - Targeted Interventions should be provided to an additional 15% of students who fall below grade level skills in the classroom. These interventions should support at risk-students: Low socio-economic, English Learners, and struggling readers.

Tier 3 - Intensive Interventions should be provided to the final 5% of students. These are extremely focused interventions that may involve as few as one or two students at a time receiving instruction that is specifically suited to their specific needs. Interventions at Tier 3 are most often delivered by specialists or instructional aides with the support of school psychologists.

In some parts of the country RTI is called RTI squared or RTII. This approach to RTI emphasizes the "I" stands for both instruction and interventions, because a quality RTI approach begins with quality instruction.   Every effective intervention provided to students should be instructionally sound.

Must Do's and May Do's

In the classroom, the teacher should work every day with students who may struggle to master on their own the skills that are taught. Teachers after they have provided the basic instruction for the day should gather struggling students in a small group of 4-6 and review the concepts and check for understanding to make sure that students comprehend the concepts being taught.   So what do the other students do while the teacher is focusing attention on the small group of struggling students? The other students should be working independently on the day's classwork to practice the skills they are learning. These students should have some Must Do's or assignments that they must complete independently. At the same time, the teacher should provide one or two activities that students May Do if they finish the Must Do's requirements early.

- *Must Do's are essential assignments that students must complete*
- *May Do's are extension assignments that students can do if they complete all of the Must Do's and still have time during seatwork time.*

The May Do list helps advanced students extend their learning. Responsible students who finish the Must Do list can also help other students complete their classwork. Keeping the bulk of the students working on the Must Do and May Do lists provides the teacher time to devote attention to small group instruction for those students who are struggling.

Interventions Early and Often

RTI looks to target struggling students early and provide interventions that can improve student learning before they fall too far behind. Interventions should begin as soon as Kindergarten. Students need interventions early in their academic experience and they need more attention and time to develop the skills and strategies to succeed in school.

- *More Attention*
- *More Time*

Students who struggle to learn the alphabet pronounce the 43 phonemic sounds, or count to 20 should receive interventions by January of the year, so that they can master these skills by the end of the school year.

RTI Strategies

The most important things that classroom teachers need to succeed with RTI are effective strategies. The RTI framework means that more students who struggle (special education and English Language Learners) are plopped into the classroom. Teachers have to deal with the fact that many more students are lack grade level skills. Classroom teachers need more strategies that can serve as an effective Response to Intervention for their struggling students. Effective intervention strategies include four important elements. These elements are essential to effective RTI results and they make a difference for kids.

Elements of Effective Interventions

- *Assess learning for students* (Academic language & vocabulary)
- *Engage students in learning* (Interactions and Fun)
- *Structure language, literacy, & learning* (For all students)
- *Make meaning for students* (Negotiating knowledge with others)

As our students develop the academic language and academic vocabulary skills they will be able to access and open doors to learning for a lifetime. As they engage in activities that are effectively structured they will create personal meaning as they negotiate and transact information with others.

Processing Learning

As you go through this book, it will be beneficial for you to consider the information from a variety of perspectives. The information you read can effect on a learner level, teacher level, and on a colleague level.

Processing Information

- *Learner Level Processing* (How will this affect my students?)
- *Teacher Level Processing* (How will this affect my instruction?)
- *Colleague Level Processing* (How will this affect our school?)

When we process information from different perspectives then we retain the information better and it becomes more meaningful to us. Farrell (2000) notes the importance of reflecting on our learning,

> *"Experience itself is not actually the greatest teacher...we do not learn as much from experience as we learn from reflecting on that experience."*

Evaluative reflections can be the most powerful reflections as we compare, order, and organize our learning.

Language, Literacy, and Learning

Every student needs to know the language and develop literacy with language in order to learn effectively. The situation regarding a lack of literacy increases in concern as the amount of information to process in the world increases. Students who have experienced a culture growing up that lacks background language and concepts that prepare students for school find that they have less background knowledge that they can connect to their future learning. Researchers have noted (Williams 2004,) the paramount importance of background knowledge in the acquisition and development of general academic knowledge and content specific knowledge. Background knowledge with the language that reveals the knowledge is the number one indicator for predicting learning success in any subject (Marzano et al., 2002). Without essential language skills and literacy abilities, learning becomes an extremely difficult proposition. Consider the following 6th grade math question from an end of year test. Read the question and write down the correct answer, while also writing down your level of confidence in your answer.

Solamente queda un pedazo en que se puede construir, y el cine ocupara todo eso completamente. En esa frase, la palabra pedazo significa

A. Mucho de algo

B. Un grupo completo

C. Una seccion de tierra

D. La resulta de un chance

Answer _____   **Confidence %**_____

So how much does language affect our ability to learn and measure learning? If you don't know Spanish, then the preceding question is extremely difficult.

Imagine having to complete 75 more questions just like it. A lack of language ability can dramatically influence our desire and determination to learn.

Cracks, Gaps, & Chasms

It is difficult to sometimes see the implications that face struggling students. Students who get behind and struggle in the second grade seem to only have a few cracks in their learning that we hope will get filled. Yet, if these students do not get targeted intervention strategies to help, they will soon find that the cracks in the early elementary grades become gaps in the upper elementary grades, and if they are still neglected can turn into chasms by the time the student finishes middle school and enters high school. The following chart outlines how cracks in a student's language will inevitably manifest itself in gaps in the student's literacy and eventually in the student's learning.

Language Cracks

Literacy Gaps

Learning Chasms

What start out as cracks, in time become gaps, and finally can create chasms in learning. Again, the gaps in American education have become chasms that swallow up entire sub-group populations of students. Those sub-group populations that are the poorest are the most at risk of getting swallowed up in the chasms of functional illiteracy and a difficult life. As noted in the research, over 40% of our African American and Latino students drop-out of school and face a very uncertain future.

The Big Five for Language and Literacy

The National Reading Panel (2000) analyzed the extensive research on language and literacy and determined that the following five areas are essential for students to become effective learners.

<u>Language Fundamentals</u>

- **Phonemic Awareness**
- **Phonics**
- **Fluency**
- **Vocabulary**
- **Comprehension**

Our students in the early elementary grades need phonemic awareness, phonics, and fluency to be able to decode effectively. While all students need to continually improve their vocabulary skills in order to comprehend text and textbooks of ever increasing difficulty as the proceed through school and onto college.

Building a House of Knowledge

It is essential that every student build within themselves a house of knowledge. These knowledge structures need to be robust and strong enough to withstand the challenges of life. Like the three little pigs, many students have the big bad wolf huffing and puffing to blow down their house of knowledge. As teachers it is imperative that we make sure that every student builds a house of knowledge that has a firm foundation and a formidable framework. So what provides student's a firm foundation that they can confidently build their knowledge structures on? The simple answer is language provides the firm foundation for structuring new knowledge. Once a foundation of language is laid, then a framework of literacy can develop, and finally the finishing work of learning can complete the house. The following chart demonstrates the three parts of building knowledge structures:

House of Knowledge Structures

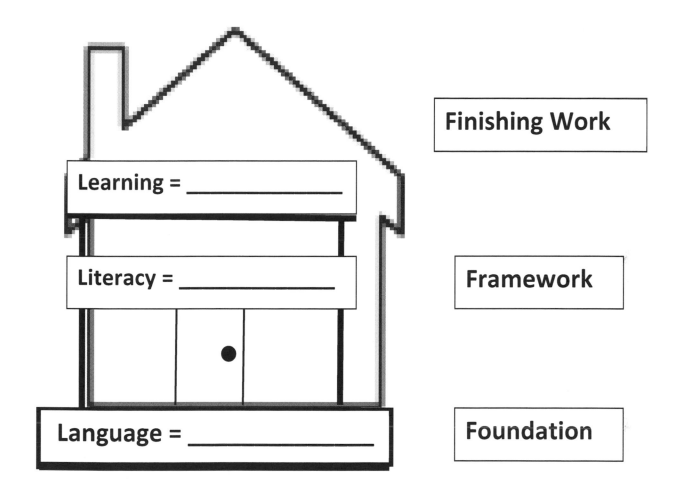

Without a foundation of academic language and a framework of academic literacy, it is very difficult for academic learning to fully develop.

Language, Literacy, & Learning

Students need the essential language and vocabulary to learn to read and to negotiate the demands off school. Having a common language allows people to communicate and share ideas. Without a common language it is difficult to interact and learn from others. Many students enter school without the language to succeed in school. The common language of school is called academic language. Those students who come to school knowing academic language typically do very well in school and they enjoy learning. The language we know determines our listening comprehension which sets the boundaries for reading comprehension. Kamil et al (2010) note that students who lack the common language of school face to difficult challenges in their academic careers:

Reading Challenges

- *The 4th grade reading slump*
- *The 7th grade reading cliff*

Language is the Foundation

So what is the foundation for learning? It's language. Language allows us to build relationships with others as well as relationships with ideas and concepts that help us learn.

Language = Relationships

Look over the following examples of academic language affecting learning relationships.

Language - Relationship Foundation

- *Sound – Symbol relationship*
- *Phonemic Awareness - Phonics relationship*
- *Word – Definition relationship*
- *Word – Picture relationship*
- *Visual Representation – Meaning relationship*
- *Prior Knowledge – Current Connection relationship*
- *Word – Sentence relationship*
- *Casual Language – Academic Language relationship*
- *Academic Language –Access Learning relationship*

Students need to learn the relationships between sounds and symbols, words and meaning, background knowledge and new connections. Comprehension for learning is greatly affected by lexical and syntactical complexity (Pearson, 2007). Lexical Complexity has to do with the complexity of vocabulary, while syntactical complexity has to do with the challenges of literacy.

Literacy is the Framework

In a democratic society, literacy is the currency for success so that an educated people can transact through reading, writing, listening, speaking, viewing, and thinking about these literacy processes and turn them into habits. Literacy can expand the network of ideas that we consider. Literacy is a process of formal communication. The United Nations Educational, Scientific and Cultural Organization (UNESCO) provides the following definition of academic literacy,

> *"Literacy is the ability to identify, understand, interpret, create, communicate and compute, using printed and written materials associated with varying contexts. Literacy involves a continuum of learning to enable an individual to achieve his or her goals, to develop his or her knowledge and potential, and to participate fully in the wider society."*

Academic literacy includes the formal educational conversations where listening, speaking, reading, and writing are effectively communicated. Traditional literacy is typically measured by learning to read. Content area literacy is measured by reading to learn and learning the language terms specific to various content areas and ultimately learning the language, concepts, and patterns of a profession.

Literacy = Negotiating

Literacy is all about negotiating, transacting, or interactions that exchange knowledge. Bearne, Dombey, and Grainger (2006) note that,

> *"Negotiating meaning and making sense are basic to all literate behavior."*

Speaking, reading, listening, and reading are essential to negotiating learning and exchanging knowledge. Students who are unable to effectively speak, read, listen, and write will invariably struggle in school. It is interesting to note that the students who struggle the most in our schools are not the poor or minorities, it is fact the deaf and the dumb. Being unable to see or hear dramatically affects one's ability to transact or exchange information. Deaf students find their learning is limited because of their limitations in transacting verbal information. Blind students can read, yet it takes a lot more time and is limited to those materials that have been tape recorded or transcribed into braille. The rate at which we can negotiate or transact knowledge affects how quickly we can learn. Consider the following aspects of Literacy and Negotiating

Literacy – Negotiating Framework

- *Knowledge Structures – Rate of connecting concepts together*
- *Reading – Negotiating meaning with the author*
- *Speaking – Transacting meaning with a known audience*
- *Listening – Negotiating meaning with the speaker*
- *Writing – Transacting meaning with an unknown audience*
- *Cognitive Learning – Interacting with meaning*

Learning is the Finishing Work

Learning is in many ways the finishing work that builds on a foundation of language and a framework of literacy. Each individual student organizes their learning to suit their particular needs. Like building a house, finishing work picks out the colors, puts up the dry wall, and selects the fixtures. Learning determines the final organization, look and feel of the house.

Learning = Organizing

As students learn they organize the input and new information in ways that they can remember it and use it in future situations.

Learning – Organizing Finishing Work

- *Organizing - Compare/Contrast Learning*
- *Organizing - Cause/Effect Learning*
- *Organizing - Problem /Solution Learning*
- *Organizing - Chronological Sequence Learning*

- *Organizing – Description Learning*
- *Organizing - Classification*
- *Hierarchy of Knowledge*
- *Knowledge Patterns*

Intervention Strategy #2: Sound Muncher/Math Monster

This intervention strategy can be used on a regular basis to review basic language facts or math facts. Begin by going to the Dollar Store or Office Depot and purchasing a small garbage can. Work with other teachers to design and create your personal Sound Munch and/or Math Monster. Once you have decorated the Sound Muncher with eyes, mouth, and other decals, you will want to make laminated cards that focus on the language-relationship skills that all students need. The list below provides a few examples of letter or word cards that can be created to practice isolated phonemes, rhymes, letters, words, etc.

Language - Relationship Foundation

- *Sound – Symbol relationship*
- *Blending*
- *Rhyming*
- *Word – Picture relationship*
- *Segmenting*
- *Onset-Rime*
- *Word – Sentence relationship*

Picture: Sound Muncher for developing language foundation

As your students successfully answer the basic language facts, they get to place the card inside the Sound Muncher. Students love being rewarded for correct answer by inserting the cards they answered correctly into the Sound Munchers mouth. Students can literally engage in this strategy every day and still enjoy the positive reward recognition for getting answers correct. If a student does not answer a card correctly then the card goes to the bottom of the deck and is reviewed. This small group activity moves quickly and is a lot of fun to do for both teacher and student alike.

Intervention Strategy #2: Fist-to-Five Vocabulary

So how can we effectively determine the level of vocabulary students bring with them to school? We need a quick and effective assessment strategy for determining what vocabulary students know and which vocabulary words they will need additional help and attention. The following strategy is essential to building the key vocabulary students need to succeed in school (adapted from Johnson & Karns, 2010)

Fist-to-Five Vocabulary Assessment

1. *I have never heard of the word before.*
2. *I've heard of the word, but I am unsure what it means.*
3. *I recognize the word, and I think it means...*
4. *I know the word in one context—it means...*
5. *I know the word in several different contexts!*

Fist-to-Five engages all learners, because they get to kinesthetically demonstrate their knowledge. This strategy is quick and easy to use. Students should engage in the Fist-to-Five vocabulary strategy every day. As students assess and show their knowledge of 5-7 words a day they will be able to quickly identify words they know as well as words they need to add to their understanding. This strategy helps learners think meta-cognitively about their own comprehension of key vocabulary words.

This book will identify differences between the language of specific academic disciplines and the language of content area learning in mathematics, language arts, science, and social studies that will develop a robust general academic register as well as specific academic discipline language.

Reflection Questions

1. *What concept or strategy are you most excited about from the first chapter?*
2. *How are intervention strategies implemented and RTI organized at your school?*

Notes

Chapter Two:

Academic Language &

Academic Vocabulary

*"The art of teaching is the
Art of self-discovery."*

Mark Van Doren

Miguel looked at the test staring at him from his desk. He looked at it again and wondered if he would ever figure it out. He reflected back when he came to America three years ago and how different life had become. He didn't always go to school in Mexico. He missed a few days here or a week or two there and it seemed like it was no big deal to anyone. Now he went to school most every day, and it was difficult learning in English. He spoke the language okay, but so many of the words in the textbooks and on the tests overwhelmed him. So much of it just didn't make sense. It was enough to make him want to quit. He looked back at question number #3 and read it again. He knew most of the words, but there were two or three that he didn't know. It seemed it was this way for every question on the test. Those couple of words made all the difference between really knowing what the question was asking. It felt like he was just guessing, so why go through the hassle of trying to decipher every question. He decided he would do his best, but his confidence was definitely shaken. He wondered if he would ever feel good as a learner.

When Does the Achievement Gap Begin?

The research from Hart and Risley (2003) sheds tremendous light on the issues at the root of the achievement gap. We know that language affects literacy, and literacy affects learning, yet how come we consistently see students from poverty struggling academically. We know that a primary indicator that influences academic success is socio-economic background. Yet, why does how much money someone has affect their educational success? It seems like generational poverty has a tremendous grip on so many students. Well Hart and Risley did their research in Kansas City, Missouri. They were socio-linguists who were interested in the interaction of languages within families. They decided to do a study where they would go into people's homes and tape record all of the conversations that occurred within the family. They went into low socio-economic homes of folks, who were on welfare, working-class homes of folks who were blue-collar and high socio-economic homes of white-collar professors. They did a longitudinal study over four years where they taped and transcribed hundreds of hours of conversations between parents and their young children. They were unsure what they were looking for exactly, yet as they analyzed the data they were fascinated with the results. As linguists they found that the vocabulary of the different kids varied dramatically and consistently. Students from low-socio-economic homes only knew half the words than similar aged students from high socio-economic homes. Here is what research from Hart & Risley (2003) reveals.

By age 3: Number of Words in Children's vocabulary	
Children from welfare families:	500 words
Children from working class families:	700 words
Children from professional families:	1100 words

So by age three there is already a tremendous gap in children's vocabulary that impacts the rate at which they can grasp new knowledge. While it is easy to point the finger at the grade level below us for students that come to us behind academically, the language gap that directly affects the achievement gap begins way before the students even come to school.

Vocabulary Size and Learning Capacity

Vocabulary is the cheap and easiest way to assess knowledge. For example, the quickest Intelligent Quotient (IQ) tests use vocabulary to measure IQ scores. Vocabulary is such a powerful indicator of concept knowledge that it also works for assessing knowledge at the college level. Have you ever taken the Graduate Requisite Exam (GRE) to get into grad school? The GRE is a standard test for assessing a college graduate's ability to handle the rigors of a Master's program. If you look at the composition of questions on the GRE you will find that over 60% or approximately two-thirds of the test is vocabulary. The test assumes that if you have an extensive vocabulary and know the definitions for the vocabulary that you will be able to succeed in grad school. While the GRE does not measure our cognitive abilities, vocabulary tests can measure our concept knowledge which has a high correlation with academic success. Again, academic language and academic vocabulary are strong indicators of academic success, because words are the building blocks that allow us to construct new knowledge. The more words we know, then the faster we can organize and construct new knowledge structures.

Why is there an Achievement Gap?

Hart and Risley were amazed by the tremendous gap in vocabulary that existed by age three and the size of the gap continued unless there were strategic interventions that were provided students. The researchers wanted to know why the gap happened so consistently between low, middle, and high socio-economic homes. So they went back to their research and analyzed the previous four-year's worth of data and began recognizing a pattern. They found that the primary factor that affected a child's vocabulary was the quantity and the quality of input they received from their parents. Children from low socio-economic homes were talked to less frequently than children from high socio-economic homes. The input of language by parents dramatically affected the output of language by their children. The research Hart & Risley (2003) showed an amazing correlation:

(Hart & Risley, 2003)	Words heard per hour	Words heard in a 100-hour week	Words heard in a 5,200 hour year	Words heard over a 4-year period
Welfare	616	62,000	3 million	13 million
Working-Class	1,251	125,000	6 million	26 million
Professional	2,153	215,000	11 million	45 million

The bottom line is that three times the input from parents equaled double the output from students. What can we learn from this? Students who come from low socio-economic homes need strategic interventions that should begin as early as kindergarten and really even before the children enter formal schooling. At the same time most students from high socio-economic homes have the vocabulary foundation to help them succeed academically in school.

Intervention Strategy #4: Structured Discussions

Our students need more time engaging in content area discussions. Many students come to school without the ability to engage effectively in conversations with their teacher or their peers. For English language students the research shows that these students actively avoid speaking English in class. Girard & Spycher (2007) note the amount of time EL students speak English class is usually very little.

Percent of Time EL Students get to speak English

- **4% of time is spent speaking Casual English**
- **2% of time is spent speaking Academic English**

All of our students need more opportunities to speak about concepts in class, yet many of them need to be explicitly taught how to engage in these types of classroom conversations. Francis et al (2006) notes that,

"Ideally, teachers would plan for structured opportunities to practice language, model effective questioning and conversational practices, and gradually turn over the responsibility to students for peer-led discussions and conversations."

Let's look at the essential skills used in this strategy. Many students may come to school without knowing how to express an opinion, ask for clarification, or paraphrase another student's response, because this has never been modeled for them at home. Here are the key components of a structured discussion.

Structured Discussion Skills

- *Paraphrasing*
- *Asking for Clarification*
- *Soliciting a Response*
- *Acknowledging others Ideas*
- *Reporting a Partner's Ideas*
- *Reporting a Group's Ideas*
- *Offering a Suggestion*
- *Agreeing*
- *Disagreeing Politely*
- *Holding the Floor*

As we help students engage frequently in structured discussions the learning environment in our classroom will improve. Langer (2001) observes,

"In the higher performing schools, at least 96% of the teachers helped students engage in the thoughtful dialogue we call shared cognition. Teachers expected

their students to not merely work together, but to sharpen their understandings with, against, and from each other."

The structured discussion sentence frames get student dialogue started in the right direction and keeps them engaged in effective discourse (adapted from Kinsella, 2007).

Paraphrasing

- ❖ So you are staying that . . .
- ❖ In other words, you think . . .
- ❖ What I hear you saying is . . .

Asking for Clarification

- ❖ What do you mean by . . .
- ❖ Will you explain that again . . .
- ❖ I have a question about that . . .

Soliciting a Response

- ❖ What do you think?
- ❖ We haven't heard from you yet.
- ❖ Do you agree with this?

Acknowledging Others Ideas

- ❖ My idea is similar to/related to_____'s idea . . .
- ❖ I agree with _____ that . . .
- ❖ My idea builds upon _____'s Idea . . .

Reporting a Partner's idea

- ❖ _____ pointed out to me that . . .
- ❖ _____ emphasized that . . .
- ❖ _____ concluded that . . .

Reporting a Group's idea

- ❖ We decided / agreed that . . .
- ❖ We concluded that . . .
- ❖ Our group believes . . .

Disagreeing

- ❖ I don't' agree with you, because . . .
- ❖ I got a different answer than you . . .
- ❖ I see it differently . . .

Offering a Suggestion

- ❖ Maybe we could . . .
- ❖ What if we . . .
- ❖ Here's something we might try . . .

Agreeing

- ❖ I like your idea about . . .
- ❖ I hadn't thought of that . . .
- ❖ I see what you mean . . .

Holding the Floor

- ❖ As I was saying . . .
- ❖ If I could finish my thought . . .
- ❖ What I was trying to say was . . .

We need to plan and organize classroom discussions, whether they are large-group or small group discussions, in ways that structure the thinking and conversations in ways which will engage students in using academic language. The structured discussion sentence frames can be typed or written out on 4 x 6 cards so that students can read the cards while they engage in content discussions.

Positive Conversations

Over time, children in welfare homes would hear twice as many negative comments from their parents compared to positive comments would hear, while children in working-class homes would hear twice as many positive comments compared to negative comments. In professional homes, children would hear over six times more positive comments compared to negative comments and the total number of words spoken to children more than doubled the number of words communicated in a welfare home. The consistent positive feedback also seemed to carry over into areas of social adjustment at school for these students in the form of higher expectations and personal aspirations. Tough (2008) summarizes the importance of language,

> *"They found that a child's experience of language mattered more than socio-economic status, more than race, more than anything else they measured."*

Their research shows we need encourage and engage our students as we help them develop the language and literacy skills needed to make up any poor hand they may have been dealt. Without explicit instruction and support, the students who lack academic language and literacy will get further and further behind each year. By the time students hit third and fourth grade when "reading to learn" becomes essential for keeping pace, the differences start to become ever more apparent.

Actual Differences in Affirmations Heard Each Year	
Welfare homes:	**26,000 affirmations and 57,000 discouragements**
Working-class homes:	**62,000 affirmations and 36,000 discouragements**
Professional homes:	**166,000 affirmations and 26,000 discouragements**
(Hart & Risley, 2003)	

Intervention Strategy #5: Easy Button Facts

The Easy Button strategy is similar to the Sound Muncher that is used in Grades K-6. The Easy Button can be used in grades K-12. Students when they get correct answers on basic language, math, science, social studies, or any content area facts are able to push the Easy Button. Kinesthetically pushing the Easy Button provides a positive reinforcement for students for every fact they answer correctly.

Students enjoy the opportunity to push the button and get an immediate response when they are correct. The following Math Facts can be reviewed using the Easy Button or the Math Monster that was discussed in the previous chapter.

Math - Facts Foundation

- *Number Sense*
- *Counting*
- *Addition*
- *Grouping Numbers*
- *Subtraction*
- *Multiplication*
- *Division*
- *Fractions*
- *Algebraic Math Facts*

Academic Language & Academic Vocabulary

As students review and master the basic facts they can then develop a stronger foundation for adding more complex literacy and learning processes.

Academic Comprehension

If we are to adequately address the achievement gap then we must begin by making sure that all students have the academic language and academic vocabulary to succeed in school. Simply stated, those students who have a robust vocabulary will do well academically, while those who lack essential vocabulary knowledge will struggle throughout their educational careers and into the future. In order to reverse the effects off a language gap and the achievement gap, we must work together to provide our students with the essential words for learning. The following chart shows how academic language is essential to go from decoding to comprehension.

Framework for Reading

DECODING *Learning to Read*			COMPREHENSION *Reading to Learn*	
Word Recognition Strategies		Fluency	Academic Language	Comprehension Strategies
Concepts of Print	Phonemic Awareness	Phonics	Sight Words	Automaticity	Background Knowledge	Brick & Mortar Vocabulary	Syntax & Text Structure	Comprehension Monitoring	(Re)organizing text

Adapted from John Shelfbine/Developmental Studies Center

Concepts of Print | Phonemic Awareness | Phonics | Sight Words | Automaticity | Background Knowledge | Brick & Mortar Vocabulary | Syntax & Text Structure | Comprehension Monitoring | (Re)organizing text

Without academic language our students will struggle and get even further and further behind in school.

Bricks and Mortar

As the book progresses through subsequent chapters the use of the term academic language will refer to the mortar that binds, ties, and holds learning together in comprehensible ways. Whenever the aspects of academic language which are discipline specific are noted in the upcoming chapters of the book, they will be referred to as academic vocabulary. The major emphasis of the book will be on the general academic language that makes up the mortar for uniting and integrating learning processes and the specific academic vocabulary that makes up the bricks of learning.

- *Bricks* (*Academic Vocabulary in subject areas like Mathematics, Language Arts, Music, Social Science, Chemistry, etc.*)

- *Mortar* (*Academic Language that serves as the glue to hold the bricks together like actions, transitions, and big concepts*)

When each of us takes the time to ensure that our students know the academic terminology they will develop more comprehension of important concepts. As students are given a variety of opportunities to apply the language and vocabulary in a pattern that is both relevant and rigorous then learning processes make sense to the learner and internal engagement increases.

Academic Vocabulary (Bricks)

The top teachers of content area literacy practices are themselves able to converse and interact with others in qualitatively higher thinking, speaking, reading, and writing. These experienced instructors think like scientists, mathematicians, historians, and other specialists, and they create a culture in their classroom that operates at a higher level. This culture created by the teacher through language and patterns of practice provides the framework for developing the next generation literate leaders. Mathematics, Language Arts, Science, and Social Studies serve as the four cornerstones of a firm academic foundation. Most states provide clear curriculum expectations in these four content areas. Formal assessments in mathematics, language arts, science, and social studies are common across the nation. State standards emphasize these four content areas, yet academic language is an integral part of all content areas in school. Although specific examples and strategies are provided in mathematics, language arts, science, and social studies, academic language can certainly be applied to all content areas in the school. The process of instruction in academic literacy can benefit the content specific literacy of all subject areas. Students with a larger academic language vocabulary consistently do better than those that have a limited academic language vocabulary. Here are the core subject areas that are assessed in most states—the chapters in the back of the book provide specific academic vocabulary bricks for students to learn.

Academic Vocabulary Bricks

- *Social Science Bricks (i.e. government, economy, geography, history, etc.)*
- *Mathematics Bricks (i.e. fraction, division, algebra, Y-axis, compute, etc.)*
- *Science Bricks (i.e. physics, biology, photosynthesis, brain, chemistry, etc.)*
- *Language Arts Bricks (i.e. plot, genre, interjection, characterization, etc.)*

As our students learn the essential academic vocabulary terms and concepts, the better they will understand various subjects and succeed in school. Pimm (1987) recognized that the language discourse in mathematics is formed from specific features of dialogue. Short (1994) takes note of the specific language functions in social studies classes. Language in social studies is centered on justifying behavior. Bailey, Butler, Stevens, and Lord (2007) found that an analysis of textbooks confirms these different benefits. Douglas (2000) in working with ELL adults noted the importance of students acquiring discipline specific knowledge and academic vocabulary. Nippold (1995) notes the variety of specific language settings students experience as they are exposed to different academic disciplines in secondary grades.

Academic Language

Academic language is the life-blood of formal schooling. The life-blood of academic language provides oxygen and nutrients to the life of the learner.

Academic literacy is the heart of education. As the heart of learning, academic literacy pumps the life blood of academic language throughout the body of knowledge within a school and within individual learners. Ensuring that the heartbeat of literacy is strong within every student in class should be the objective of every teacher. If schools struggle to provide their students with the academic language to engage their students in academic concept development, and to generate within their students the academic patterns of learning, then many students will slowly lose their academic pulse. With so many learners slowly becoming anemic to academic language, we find so many students entering high school experiencing academic arrest. For students of poverty and color the numbers are alarming. Without a transfusion of several pints of academic language development then academic arrest may be imminent. Academic language includes the socio-linguistic aspects-Schleppelgrell, grammatical aspects-Scarcella, and the vocabulary aspects-Marzano. Yet, the socio-linguist aspect of language purposes can be confusing for a new second grade teacher, and definitely for a new second grade student. The grammatical and vocabulary aspects can be overwhelming as well. So let's look at the essential components of academic language. We have already noted the difference between the bricks and mortar of academic language, and we have outlined several of the key subjects that make up the bricks. Now let's consider the three key aspects of the academic language mortar. Just as real mortar has three parts (sand, water, & cement) academic mortar has three parts. The three parts of academic language mortar is:

Academic Language Mortar

- *Action Words* (*Identify, Compose, Analyze, Examine, Apply, Do*)
- *Transition Words* (*Because, Whenever, If…then, After, As a result*)
- *Concept Words* (*Evidence, Strategy, Process, Analysis, Component*)

The specific content language is what separates the various academic disciplines into different content areas. The type of academic language that integrates education is the general academic language that unites the different ways our minds think about the world. Reading and writing are the two typical measurements for literacy in the world. Academic reading and academic writing consist of more than just reading a newspaper or writing a letter to a friend. Academic reading includes being able to negotiate the challenges of today's textbooks that are increasing in their rigor and the amount of academic language. Developing formal written communication is a skill that so many students today lack. Academic writing includes being able to construct communication for analytical essays, research papers, and technical reports. Academic reading and writing covers the complex abilities that will help students succeed at school, at college, and in the professional world. Academic language provides the means to understand and effectively communicate the actions, transitions, and relationships between the types of knowledge that are valued at school.

Improving Academic Language Knowledge

As teacher-leaders, academic coaches, and classroom teachers work together to improve academic language and literacy, we will be able to improve the academic foundation and framework that will support student learning now and in the future. Academic language can serve as a unifying foundation when creating an academic culture within a classroom and throughout a school. The instructional leaders at school can generate greater academic results as they develop a culture of learning around academic language and align and integrate academic literacy for every student. In the Institute of educational sciences report (IES) by the U.S. Department of Education Gersten et al (2007) provide a couple of recommendations for effective literacy instruction for English Language Learners which can benefit all struggling students:

- **Recommendation 3**: Provide extensive and varied vocabulary instruction
- **Recommendation 4:** Develop Academic English

Within recommendation three the **IES report** says to,

"Develop district-wide lists of essential words for vocabulary instruction. These words should be drawn from the core reading program and from the textbooks used in key content areas, such as science and history."

This report highlights the need for vocabulary instruction in the specific content language of different disciplines. Districts should use a quality program of instruction that will provide a comprehensive system for vocabulary development. Recommendation four of the **IES report** emphasizes the importance of providing instruction in the words, functions, and structures of general academic language. As teachers add quality instruction in the general academic language and improve their instruction in the specific content language vocabulary then English Language Learners and all students will see crucial long term benefits in their academic and future careers.

Intervention Strategy #6: Academic Vocabulary Graphic Organizer

There are a variety of methods that work well when explicitly teaching academic vocabulary. This strategy introduces the Johnson Academic Vocabulary Graphic Organizer. There are seven parts to this academic vocabulary graphic organizer.

Academic Vocabulary Graphic Organizer

1. *Write down the word*
2. *List synonyms*
3. *List examples*
4. *Write down a working definition*
5. *Draw a picture*
6. *List antonyms*
7. *List non-examples*

Each of the seven parts of the graphic organizer assist students in learning key vocabulary words in-depth. The most difficult parts of the graphic organizer are the non-examples and antonyms. Once a student writes down their own working definition, draw a picture, and list non-examples they typically own the word and are confident using it in speaking and writing. The following graphic organizer can help students develop mastery of the key academic words they need to know.

Academic Vocabulary Graphic Organizer

Students should fill out the academic vocabulary graphic organizer for selected words from the 75 academic language word list, 75 social studies word list, 75 mathematics word list, 50 science word list, and 50 language arts word list. The following chart shows a graphic organizer filled in. Academic language has a potential strength and a potential weakness. Academic language operates differently and expects different things from the learner depending on the content discipline involved. For example analysis in language arts may look very different than analysis in mathematics, science, or social studies. In language arts one may analyze characters, plot patterns, or figurative language. In mathematics one may analyze equations, algebraic processes, geometric angles, or functional properties. In science one may analyze chemical components, atomic structure, energy forces, or photosynthesis processes. In social studies one may analyze political parties, religious beliefs, economic systems, or social barriers. Analyzing these various disciplines requires very different abilities and students may demonstrate an aptitude for one type of analysis and struggle with a different type of analysis. The strength of mastering academic language is that when a student can analyze in multiple disciplines their understanding and mastery of the process and the content increases significantly.

Academic Language Graphic Organizer

Johnson Model

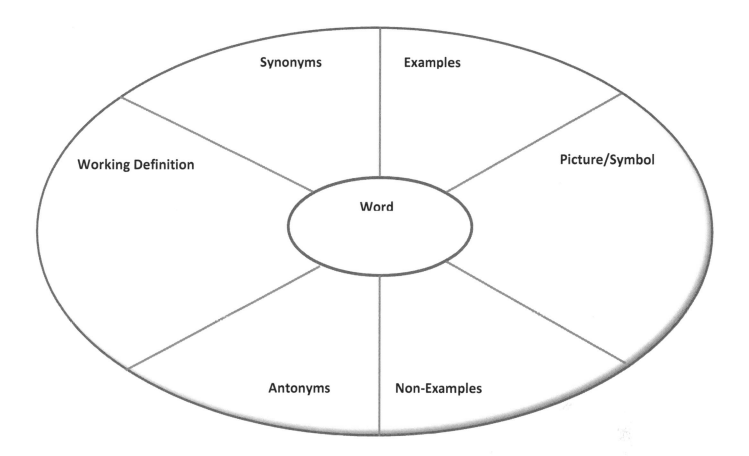

new words and process them in their mind. As students compare and contrast, consider a working definition, make a mental picture, and identify examples and non-examples they will be much more effective at adding new words to their vocabulary.

Intervention Strategy #7: Language Registers

The ability to use language registers effectively in academic settings increases the ease with which conceptual connections can be created and retained by students. Language registers consist of the key vocabulary that sets apart different social groups and the interactions that make up the social settings. Language registers can be separated into three primary areas:

Language Registers

- *Casual Language Registers (Hobbies, Personal Interests, Conversations with Friends and Family)*
- *Academic Language Registers (Curriculum, Instruction, & Assessment Language, Language of Formal Writing, Academic Language, Academic Vocabulary)*
- *Professional Language Registers (Job Vernacular, Professional Conversations, Work Jargon)*

As struggling students receive more attention and more time, then more students will be able to achieve grade level standards and expectations (Brown-Chidsey & Cummings, 2007).

Language Register Learning

Language Register	Years Needed to Learn
Casual Language	1 to 2 years
Academic Language	7 to 10 years

Students who develop a casual language register will be better prepared to learn academic language registers, and academic language registers prepare students for professional language registers.

Academic Language is a Language of Execution

Academic language is a challenging language to learn, because it expects much of the person operating within the language. Academic language instead of being passive is extremely active. Academic language requires a lot of actions and effort of learners. Communication of any kind expects something of the recipient of the language. Even if the expectation is just to listen and understand. Academic Language has much greater expectations.

Academic language requires learners to *define, analyze, examine, compare, synthesize, execute* etc. Note that EL students can learn the casual language register of the playground, hallway, and neighborhood, but they struggle in school because they can't negotiate the demands of the classroom. It often takes EL students five to seven years before they begin to effectively develop an academic language register, if they in fact ever do develop an academic language register. Specific intervention strategies can increase the achievement level of EL students as well as other students from poverty that lack an academic language register. As a result these students are typically anywhere from two to four years behind their academic peers.

Casual Language Registers

Negotiating the language challenges of the classroom can seem far more difficult for many inner-city youth than negotiating the street rap of the corner neighborhood. This casual language helps them interact with peers in lunch lines, yet it falls far short of providing these students the ability to negotiate the textbooks, assessments, and learning demands which contain a high level of academic language. Payne (2005) notes many of the differences between the types of language use in homes of students in poverty in contrast to the language use in middle class homes.

Casual Language Registers Examples

- *Sports Talk (Fantasy Football Leagues, Basketball, Wresting, etc.)*
- *Hobbies (Quilting, Cooking, Chess, Gardening, Sky Diving, etc.)*
- *Texting (LOL, BFF, 4ever, CM, BBBG, CUL8R, NTK etc.)*

The language of common discourse is dramatically different than the language of academic discourse. Students will communicate for long hours via text messaging, emailing, blogging, phone calls, and viewing and interacting with webpages on websites like MySpace and Facebook. The language of school which is comprised primarily of general academic language and specific content language is an entirely different language. Students can learn second languages. If you look at the language structure of text messaging with its acronyms, abbreviations, and new terminology, it is easy to recognize that it is an entirely different language. The language of text messaging is a language that is rich in context. The language of academics is a context that is initially challenging to most every student, yet it is completely foreign to many students from poverty. Socio-economically disadvantaged students communicate with a casual language that works great on the streets, yet it poorly prepares them for the academic rigors of courses that will prepare them for work. Many students feel that they lack the language structures to succeed in school.

Professional Language Registers

Each profession has a language register that sets the profession apart. Have you ever had a conversation with a family member or friend about their job and they use jargon that is sometimes difficult to follow? Have you ever rambled about school and thrown out several academic acronyms that the listener was unable to understand. We talk about our profession and often use language and vocabulary that others do not fully understand. Knowing the language register of a specific profession is important for succeeding in that profession. I know that I have gone into job interviews and tossed out a variety of acronyms and school jargon like PLC, RTI, IEP, and ZPD to express my professional knowledge. We are often taking for granted the amount of conceptual knowledge that these words and language registers convey. It is important to note that the academic language registers of school prepare us for learning the professional language registers of work.

Professional Language Registers

- *Dentist (Drill, X-ray, Braces, Bicuspid, Flouride, Amalgam, etc.)*
- *Plumber (Snake, Wrench, Valve, Siphon, Flange, Elbow, etc.)*
- *Hydrologist (Aquifer, Crest, Dam, Ablation, Erosion, Run off, etc.)*
- *Attorney (Case, Affidavit, Continuance, Jurisdiction, Sidebar, etc.)*

Johns (1997) identifies that each profession has a professional language register with unique language dynamics that are closely linked to different academic disciplines. So, fully developing the various specific academic language abilities of students can significantly support the development of specific professional language registers. Academic language disciplines prepare students for the specific professional language registers for greater success in college and career. Going back to school to get up to speed on new building codes for plumbers, new computer chips or equipment for auto mechanics, or new skills for electricians is the current reality. These are good jobs that provide a good living. These hands-on occupations require certification and re-certification. In these trades the academic language is replaced by occupational languages. These jobs expect future workers to understand occupational concepts that can more easily be grasped if students already have understanding of academic concepts. The patterns of occupational success repeated again and again until they become habits have greater opportunity for development if academic patterns are already in place. Professions use the abstraction action language of academic language. When a student comes home and asks for help from a parent who lives and knows the language of their profession, the parents can give help and support. They can easily explain in detail, give examples of ways to approach the question, provide partial answers and let their student fill in the rest, give analogies etc. All of the things the teacher would do if they were readily available to give additional insight, instruction, and support.

Academic Language

Academic language registers are important for succeeding in most every aspect of school. Student need to recognize that continuing education and being comfortable with the academic language of learning that exists in elementary, middle, and high school and continues at an advanced level in our nation's colleges and universities. Academic language is the hidden requirement that affects students in a multitude of ways. Consider the following areas of school that are affected by academic language.

Academic Language Areas of Influence

- *Curriculum*
- *Explicit Instruction*

- *Formal Assessments*
- *Common Core Standards*
- *School Textbooks*
- *Higher Order Thinking & Writing*
- *College and Higher Education*

As our students learn academic language they will be more successful in all aspects of their schooling.

Academic Language and Socio-Economic Background

The types of conversations and breadth of language used in many homes creates a potential divide that places many students at a significant literacy disadvantage before they even enter school. Peter S. Jennison (1998) highlights the disparity between the language registers of poor students and affluent students.

> *"The poor and the affluent are not communicating because they do not have the same words. When we talk of the millions who are culturally deprived, we refer not to those who do not have access to good libraries and bookstores, or to museums and centers for the performing arts, but those deprived of the words with which everything else is built, the words that open doors. Children without words are licked before they start. The legion of the young wordless in urban and rural slums, eight to ten years old, do not know the meaning of hundreds of words which most middle-class people assume to be familiar to much younger children."*

The American dream of entering the land of opportunity confident and prepared is marred by the fact so many of our youth have opted out of getting a diploma which serves as a ticket to future opportunities in college and career. High school drop-out rates are increasing and affect low socio-economic students the most. These students need to develop academic language, so that they can avoid the achievement gap and meet grade level standards. Research shows that teachers who have acquired a greater verbal ability in academic language produce greater achievement among their students (Stronge, 2007).

Academic Language is a Second & Third Language

Academic language is a second language for virtually all learners who attend school. A child's life outside of school typically is engaged in casual conversations and playful activities. Using precise academic language with precision and accuracy is an activity that few children experience outside of school activities. Academic language differs from casual language For English language learners academic language is a third language. The English language learner has their language of origin, conversational English language, and then academic language of school. Obtaining mastery of conversational English is a significant accomplishment. (Hill & Flynn, 2006) and (Haynes, 2007) outline the specific concerns that are faced by so many of America's Latino population as English Language Learners. It makes sense, students who are learning English as their second language would have difficulty in actively generating an academic language, academic concepts, and academic patterns in the English language. Yet, the research shows that so many primary English learners of poverty and special education background lack the same academic language, academic concepts, and academic patterns.

Summarizing Academic Language

So let's review the how much academic language impacts learning for our students. Academic language is essential for students even before they enter school and becomes more important for them every year they remain in school. When a learner is presented academic language across the curriculum, multiple opportunities to develop academic concepts, and challenging activities that engage academic patterns then the learner is provided a mental framework for building meaningful learning. The learner better understands the relationships between concepts and courses while the relationship between teacher and learner is also enhanced. The learner better sees the relevance for learning as different courses are integrated as well as the relevance of their learning to real world applications for now and in the future. Lastly, the learner is provided the foundation, background knowledge, and academic processes to more fully be engaged in activities that require academic rigor.

As we wrap up this chapter let's take one more shot at the 6ᵗʰ grade math question from the end of year exam. This time half of the question is in English and all of the answers are in English. See how it goes with the additional help.

Let's Try It Again

Only remains *un pedazo en* question *se puede construir, y el* theater occupied all *eso* space.

En ese **sentence, the word** *pedazo* **means**

A. a great amount.

B. a complete group.

C. a section of land.

D. a result of chance.

Answer _____   **Confidence %** _____

Aligning Instruction

Aligning curriculum with the instruction in the classroom and then aligning the instruction to the assessment helps to connect the content, the process, and the evaluation of schooling. As students are able to see how the content of their learning aligns with the learning processes and the final assessments of school, then learning becomes more relevant. When each teacher in a school takes the time to ensure that students know the academic language to develop multiple understandings of concepts and are given a variety of opportunities to apply the word in a pattern that is both relevant and rigorous, then learning processes make sense to the student and internal engagement increases. Academic language needs to be explicitly taught and learned at school. The vast majority of casual vocabulary words are picked up in casual conversations and through other mediums of communication like the television or the radio. Academic language is learned in academic settings through explicit, purposeful, and systematic instruction. Explicit instruction and literacy activities should be specifically structured to help all students learn. Explicit instruction in the modes of literacy specifically includes engaging students in the following areas: speaking, listening, reading, writing, and viewing.

Intervention Strategy #8: Concept Posters

Concept posters are a great way to engage students as they summarize and meta-cognitively review the key concepts they have learned. Concept posters can be used in any classroom for any subject. This strategy can be done individually or preferably with groups of three or four students. There are five key steps for creating effective concept posters.

Steps for Creating Concept Posters

- **Use at least Four Colors**
- **Include a Border for the Poster**
- **Highlight, Underline, and Bold Key Concepts**
- **Use good handwriting**
- **Draw Pictures that symbolize the Concepts**

Once students create their posters on the concepts being covered in class, they should present a 1-2 minute overview of the key concepts to the rest of the class. This provides a great review for all students of the key concepts. After the presentations, the posters should be prominently displayed throughout the room.

Reflection Questions

1. *How do you explicitly ensure that all of your students have the grade-level academic language they need to succeed in school?*
2. *What strategies do you use to helps students learn academic language and literacy?*

Notes

Chapter Three:
Intervention Strategies for
Student Comprehension

"A mind once stretched by a new idea,
Never regains its original dimensions."

Oliver Wendell Holmes

Rudy looked over his homework and struggled to come up with the answers. Reading had become a chore. He enjoyed reading time around the rug with his kindergarten teacher, but reading in seventh grade wasn't nearly as fun. No one stopped to explain the pictures anymore; in fact there were very few pictures in the textbooks Rudy had to read. All of the responsibility for deciphering the textbook was on him, and it was a struggle. Rudy avoided reading any books as a general rule, and was down-right resistant to reading textbooks. It was difficult to learn without reading the textbooks in class, but it seemed like a waste of time to read. Half of the time it seemed like after reading a page that he had no idea what the page said. He could read the words, but he didn't really understand what was being talked about. School seemed less and less fun. He thought about life outside of school. He didn't see himself doing anything that involved reading. He wondered why reading was so hard. He was unsure yet, but he figured reading just wasn't for everyone—at least he felt it wasn't for him.

Comprehension

Comprehension is a process of enlightenment. Comprehension begins in so many ways with self-awareness, and it increases our ability to understand others. Everyone wants to comprehend themselves and to be understood by others. Comprehension occurs when we connect ideas together, whether these ideas are our own or the ideas of others. Digging into comprehension can develop deeper understanding. Understanding creates an appreciation for others and our own unique differences. When we connect with other individuals and their intelligent ideas, then our comprehension increases. Comprehension gives us the knowledge to determine future direction in our own lives. Comprehension encourages us to pursue purposes for ourselves and gives us the understanding to make promises to others. It is an amazing quality that as human beings we are able to comprehend language. Language defines us and the world around us. Uncovering the formal language of education reveals the academic purposes of school. So, what are the ways that academic language is infused in our schooling? The words of academic language are inextricably linked to success in school through the *processes* of learning, the *functions* of learning, and the *experiences* of learning. When academic language is at the center of the instructional process, then students are better able to construct their own internal knowledge structures (Hirsch 2003). Again, an important benefit of aligning academic language systematically throughout a class, school, and district is that the terms, concepts, and patterns associated with academics consistently correlate to real world occupations and future challenges. The key components of curriculum, instruction, and assessment become more effectively understood as academic language is used consistently by teachers and effectively used by students. Moats (2000)

"Comprehension depends, firstly, on a large, working vocabulary and substantial background knowledge."

As each educator become more aware of academic language, recognize the function of academic language, and identify the structure of academic language, then the key instructional processes that generate academic literacy will become a crucial part of the school's academic culture. Let's take another quick look at the Framework for Reading that emphasizes the role Academic Language plays in developing effective comprehension strategies for our students.

Framework for Reading

DECODING Learning to Read			COMPREHENSION Reading to Learn		
Word Recognition Strategies		Fluency	Academic Language		Comprehension Strategies
Concepts of Print / Phonemic Awareness / Phonics	Sight Words	Automaticity	Background Knowledge	Brick & Mortar Vocabulary	Syntax & Text Structure / Comprehension Monitoring / (Re)organizing text

Adapted from John Shelfbine/Developmental Studies Center

Academic Reading Challenge

Let's take some time an now jump into an academic challenge. Consider the following question: *What percentage of words need to be included in a reading passage for most students to be able to infer successfully?* After you consider this question, please write down your answer here:

_____.

In the reading challenge below, read the paragraph to your best ability and as quickly as possible.

Reading Challenge!

_____ is critically _____ to the _____ of children's _____ skills and therefore to ___ ability to _____ education. Indeed, _____ _____ has come to __ the "essence of _____" (Durkin, 1993), _____ not only___ academic _____ in all subject _____ but to _____ _____ as well. In carrying out it's _____ of the extant _____ in reading _____, the NRP _____ three predominant _____ in the research on the _____ of _____ comprehension skills. First, _____ _____ is a complex cognitive _____ that cannot be understood _____ a clear description __ the ____ that _____ development and _____ _____ play in the understanding __ what has been ____. Second, _____ is an active _____ that _____ an intentional and thoughtful interaction _____ the _____ and the text. ____, the preparation of _____ to better _____ students to develop ___ apply _____ comprehension _____ to enhance _____ is intimately linked __students' achievement in this ____. Because these three _____ serve as the _____ for _____ how best to help _____ develop _____ comprehension abilities, the extant _____ relevant to vocabulary_____, to text _____ instruction, and to ___ preparation of _____ to teach reading comprehension _____ was _____ in detail ___ the NRP.

If you are up for it, read another passage from the Reading Panel's Report with fewer words missing and see how it goes.

Reading Challenge II

_Teaching _____ comprehension strategies to students at all grade levels is complex. Teachers not only ____ have a firm grasp of the content _____ in text, but also must have substantial knowledge of the strategies themselves, of which _____ are most effective for different students and types of _____ and of how best to _____ and model strategy use. Research on comprehension strategies has _____ dramatically over the last two _____. Initially, investigators focused on teaching one strategy at a time; later studies examined the effectiveness of teaching _____ strategies in combination. However, implementation of this promising _____ has been problematic. Teachers ____ be skillful in their instruction and be_ *able to respond flexibly and _____ to students' needs for instructive feedback as they read.*

You may have found that Reading Challenge II was much easier to comprehend, because 90% of the words were provided rather than 70% of the words. Students need 90% of the words in a given passage to construct effective comprehension and understanding.

Reading Strategy #8: The 90% Rule of Comprehension

At the same time that we want to be cognizant of the reality that students of poverty need extra attention and support for their academic language, we also want to expect these students to bridge the gap and let them know if they learn cognitive strategies, read at appropriate levels. We hear often that students need to read at the appropriate reading level. For someone who isn't a trained linguist o psychometric, how does the average teacher in the classroom figure this out? We come back to the 90% rule. If you can tell that the student has prior knowledge of 90% of the words in the selected reading passage, then you can be confident that the reading is at an appropriate level. We can approach this situation in two ways. We can dumb down the text and get a basic text, or we can smarten up the student by explicitly teaching academic language and specific content vocabulary. Monitoring comprehension helps students be able to infer meaning from text, and we need to monitor our student's comprehension to make sure all of our students know at least 90% of the words before we ask them to engage in reading text (Rog, 2003).

Determining Reading Levels

- *Independent Reading Level - Learners know at least 95% of the key academic language terms that are included in the reading selections for the day.*

- *Instructional Reading Level* - *Learners know 90-95% of the key academic language terms that are included in the reading selections for the day.*

- *Frustrated Reading Level* - *Learners have received little instruction, yet they know less than 90% of the key academic language terms that are included in the reading selections for the day.*

Reading and writing are the two typical measurements for literacy in the world. Academic reading and academic writing consist of more than just reading a newspaper or writing a letter to a friend. Academic reading includes being able to negotiate the challenges of today's textbooks that are increasing in their rigor and the amount of academic language. Moats (2000) adds,

"Thus the concept of independent reading level is important: it is the level at which the child recognizes more than 95 percent of the words and can read without laboring over decoding."

Francis et al. (2006) add,

"For many older learners, the focus is on words highlighted in the textbook; these word lists are often filled with rare and unusual words, such as dandelion, burrowed, or bootlegging that are not always the most important for comprehension, and can even detract from their learning. These lists don't usually include many of the high-utility academic words such as analyze or frequent, or important function words such as although and therefore."

Developing formal written communication is a skill that so many students today lack. Academic writing includes being able to construct communication for analytical essays, research papers, and technical reports. Academic reading and writing covers the complex abilities that will help students succeed at school, at college, and in the professional world. Academic reading and academic writing consist of more than just reading a newspaper or writing a letter to a friend. Academic reading includes being able to negotiate the challenges of today's textbooks that are increasing in their rigor and the amount of academic language. Academic writing includes being able to construct communication for analytical essays, research papers, and technical reports. We can follow the following three steps to help students develop the vocabulary to succeed in reading at school (adapted from Biancorosa and Snow, 2004).

1. **Pre-reading** preview important vocabulary, make predictions, identify text features, make sure students know 90% of words in reading passages

2. **While reading** notice graphic representations of concepts, ask questions, monitor comprehension of unfamiliar words

3. **Post-reading** rephrase, summarize, compare ideas with others, determine main points from details.

Are there any other ideas that can think of that will help students in pre-reading, while reading, or post-reading opportunities? Improving the results of comprehension for learners is particularly important to low-income learners who are already facing a language gap which also translates into a knowledge gap. Fluency increasing the rate, expression, and automaticity allows the learners mind to have more energy to concentrate on comprehension. Domain knowledge and specific domain language increases fluency, broadens language base, and supports deeper comprehension. This helps explain why the research shows time and time again that the amount of reading contributes significantly to the ability to learn and retain new knowledge. Stanovich (1993) outlines several steps that will help students front-load the vocabulary needed to successfully comprehend classroom reading assignments.

Reminders for the 90% Rule of Comprehension

1. Check for understanding and explicitly teach students key academic language

2. *Check for understanding and explicitly teach students specific content language*
3. *Make sure students use multiple methods for inferring meaning*
4. *Encourage students to read on their own*

Academic reading and writing covers the complex abilities that will help students succeed at school, at college, and in the professional world. Helping students develop their own abilities to infer understanding is an important part of developing effective knowledge structures. Consider the following chart (Johnson, 2009) that highlights the average number of words students from different socio-economic backgrounds learn each day:

Readers Background	Estimated number of words learned per year	Average number of words learned per day
Socio-economically disadvantaged students	3,000	7 Words
Working-class students	5,000	12 Words
Professional students	5,500	14 Words

Most of the words students learn each day are learned through the process of inferring from books or academic texts. Only 10% of new words are learned by students through the process of explicit-direct instruction. Without effective inferring skills, students will struggle to read grade-level textbooks and fully develop the skills needed to succeed in college. As a result, inferring may be the number one most important strategy for our students to learn and master.

Kids Explanations

- *"The tides are a fight between the Earth and moon. All water tends towards the moon, because there is no water in the moon, and nature abhors a vacuum. I forget where the sun joins in this fight."*
- *"Water is composed of two gins, Oxygin and Hydrogin. Oxygin is pure gin. Hydrogin is gin and water."*
- *"To keep milk from turning sour, keep it in the cow."*
- *"Germinate: To become a naturalized German."*
- *"Vacumm: A large, empty space where the pope lives."*
- *"Genetics explains why you look like your father, and if you don't, why you should."*
- *"You can listen to thunder and tell how close you came to getting hit. If you don't hear it, you got hit, so never mind."*
- *"When you breathe, you inspire. When you do not breathe, you expire."*

Intervention Strategy #9: Inferring for Content Learning

Inferencing or inferring is a matter of bridging and filling a gap in information. At the earliest levels of learning to read the students will replace a letter to change the word to a different meaning. Eventually students can begin to infer from short sentences. Eventually we want students to infer from paragraphs and between paragraphs. It is difficult to include every bit of information in the text. We write in ways that cause learners to create their own meaning from the context of the message. Actual cognitive strategies can be taught to students so that they become better at inferring from reading. The ultimate objective of the instruction process is to develop comprehension regarding the world around us. Pearson (2007) emphasizes that,

"Comprehension is relating the new to the known."

Comprehension is developed as we understand the logic structures which organize our language, and we also understand the logic structures which organize our conceptual knowledge. Inferring is the process by which we recognize the meaning of words. As we see the meaning behind individual words we can begin to understand how to connect words and phrases into comprehensible thoughts. The meaning created from words and phrases can then be linked to other phrases and clauses until we can create meaning from whole sentences. As we make meaning of individual clauses and sentences, we can then make meaning of entire paragraphs and passages. Eventually, after hundreds of inferential experiences we can make meaning of compete chapters and entire books.

Developing Comprehension and Creating Meaning

When students have even a few breakdowns in their ability to infer the meaning of specific words and the logical ideas which connect it to the phrases and sentences surrounding these words, then their ability to make sense of the paragraph or passage is limited and their comprehension is compromised. Students who can accurately decode language by recognizing sounds and fluently produce the sounds used for "learning to read" do so by reading simple easy to comprehend stories. As students progress into the upper grades of elementary school and into middle school, the importance of "reading to learn" becomes an increasingly more difficult ability to master. Students as they advance in grade levels face reading assignments and textbooks that are cognitively more difficult. Cain & Oakhill (2007) observe,

"Children with poor comprehension often fail to generate inferences to go beyond the meanings of individual sentences, to link up ideas within a text, and to incorporate their own background knowledge to make full sense of text."

It is important for learners to infer from both oral and written statements. The challenges become much bigger for learners when they engage with written text, because formal written text is more academically complex and dense. The differences learners face, when inferring from oral statements and written statements, stems from the fact that writing has much more challenging academic language and much more complex language structures compared to spoken communication. Readers who effectively increase their inferential skills are able to draw accurate conclusions and make sense of the material they read. Education has 13 years to impact this equity gap and it will take a coordinated comprehensive effort. Look over the following types of inferences and examples which highlight how inferences can be made

Six Ways to Make Inferences

* ❖ *Infer Characteristics of an Object* – *"The metal flakes in the pan of river water and sand shimmered in the sun." We might infer he found gold.*

* ❖ *Infer Time* – *"When the rooster crowed, I rolled over and smelled bacon." We might infer it is morning.*

* ❖ *Infer Action* – *"I heard a crash and crunch of metal around the corner." We might infer there was a car accident."*

* ❖ *Infer Location* – *"After looking at Abraham Lincoln we saw the Declaration of Independence and then stood in front of the White House." We might infer we are in Washington, DC.*

* ❖ *Infer Feelings/Attitudes* – *"When the professor gave Mary Ann her test back with an A+ on the front, she started jumping up and down." We might infer she was excited.*

* ❖ *Infer Causal Relationships* – *"The metal bar landed on Todd's hand, and he was rushed from shop class to the emergency room." We might infer Todd's hand is broken.*

This strategy works because it helps students develop their own ability to make important connections. The following sentences can be used to help students identify various inferences which they can make as they read.Hoy and Miskell (2002) in their study of educational administration research found that,

"Moreover, ecological research in classrooms repeatedly finds that teachers rely on just three or four instructional routines to accomplish the majority of their instructional work."

We need to expand our instructional repertoires especially in the area of academic interventions.

Sample Assignment for Developing Inferences

Read each sentence and make an inference about the possible characteristics, actions, relationships, time, feelings, or location and determine which types of inference each sentence contains.

1. The knights broke down the outside gate and stormed the castle.
2. Bob shook the can of soda pop and then opened it.
3. The river water had lots of microbes and little oxygen content.
4. Julian received a note to go to the main office.
5. We sat in the balcony munching popcorn as the previews began.
6. The teacher began with "Once upon a time.."
7. Yesterday, after we cleaned out our desks we had to take everything home.
8. Daddy divided the cookie into three equal pieces and gave one piece to Julie and two pieces to Billy.

Since the process of inferring is most often taken for granted, you will want to make transparent the thinking, inferring, and reasoning processes that your students engage in to become effective readers.

Students who can infer successfully have developed the number one skill for becoming effective comprehenders of school textbooks. As our students learn to look for multiple inferences in a given sentence or passage, they will increase their ability develop academic understanding.

Intervention Strategy #10: Comparing Text Structures

The cognitive challenges of textbooks seem to perpetually increase, because of an increase in the academic demands of language, an increase in the logical complexity of concepts, and an increase in the structural complexity of language. All of these challenges heighten the importance of increasing students' abilities to infer meaning from words and make logical connections between ideas. Students, who know academic language contained in assigned reading passages, are able to understand reading assignments more quickly and to learn key concepts more effectively. A special needs student may need a text that is more readily accessible, yet it means they need strategic and intensive intervention that will get them up to speed quickly. Learning to read and developing the abilities to read at grade level is in many ways a civil right. Kame'enui and Carnine (1998) state,

"In textbooks and other expository texts, organizational features and structures help students understand, learn from, and remember what they read. Research has shown that understanding how text is organized helps readers construct meaning."

Understanding text structure supports the creation of meaning for students.

Picture: Three students enjoying school

Let's consider the following comparison chart that addresses the differences betwee narrative and informative text (adapted from Snow, Griffin, and Burns, 2005).

Narrative Text	Informative Text
Character-oriented towards the actions of a particular character	*Subject-oriented* towards a particular topic or issue
Primary purpose: *to entertain* and to give literary or aesthetic experience	Primary purpose: *to explain*, to present information, or to persuade
Based on *life experiences* and relationship between characters	Based on *abstract concepts* and relationship between ideas
Academic language may be less essential with few new words introduced; often contains *dialogue* and many words common in spoken language	*Academic language* is essential to comprehension; introduces many content specific words and complex sentence structures
Most often employs a predictable sequenced pattern along a time line; it conveys a *beginning, middle and end* of events	Uses a *variety of text patterns*, often in the same text; i.e. compare and contrast, description, cause and effect, problem and solution, and chronological sequencing
Links the character's actions or a sequence of events in time order beginning, middle, and end	*Links relationships* between ideas from most important idea to supporting ideas with examples
Has *illustrations* that show actions of characters in colorful detail	Has *charts*, diagrams, facts, pictures, and/or tables
Reader *Questions*: "Who is the main character?"; "What happened next?"; "How did the problem get solved?"	Reader *Questions*: "What is the main subject?"; "What are the supporting details?"; "How can I use this information?"

Students need to organize their brain or the information in their brain differently as they engage with narrative and informative text. As students learn about informative text structures they will be better prepared to learn in different content-areas. Explicit instruction in text structures should include the following three strategies adapted from (Roit, 2006):

1.   *Explicitly explain different types of texts* (Compare different types)

2.   *Teach signal words to identify text structures* (linguistic clues)

3.   *Organize and generate quality writing* (Model effective writing)

One of the great concerns of students in poverty is they have language skills that are impoverished in both quantity and quality. Students in poverty enter school with less than half of the academic language of their more economically fortunate peers. Students who have less academic language when they enter school, typically see the gap in achievement widen as they go through school. Those who have sufficiently acquired academic language continue to learn at an effective and efficient rate, while those who lack academic language get further and further behind their peers as their continue their academic career. Many students, who are impoverished in their academic language, self-select out of school, because they fell overwhelmed by the ever increasing language demands of school. The gaps in their language seem so large, we see an ever increasing number of students drop out of school and face the prospects of a diminishing future. These students are searching for a way to comprehend and meet the ever increasing language demands of school. The instructional solution should start in kindergarten and systematically be infused throughout each grade level to strengthen academic language. Specific instruction in academic language that supports academic literacy is crucial to bridging the gap between students who have an enriched language and an impoverished language. In addition to scaffolding learning, giving more attention, and devoting more time to low socio-economic students, we need to provide more positive support to these students.

Reflection Questions
1. *How can you help bridge the achievement gap that affects your students at your grade-level or in your school?*
2. *As you consider the three points of view for learning, what have you learned as a learner, as a teacher, and as a colleague?*

Notes

Chapter Four:
Advanced Intervention Strategies
for Our Students

*"Kind words can be short and
easy to speak, but their
echoes are endless"*

Mother Theresa

Consuela worked with her classmates on the grade-level word lists that her teacher gave to her at the beginning of the year. There were math, science, language arts, and social studies lists. There was another list of words that seemed a little more difficult to learn. These words were challenging, yet once she understood them they helped her learn in her main subjects at school. She really liked learning the word "analyze." It seemed that this word could be used in every subject and with most anything. Consuela found herself analyzing the bus driver, the fields of crops, and the cloud patterns—really most anything. Analyzing became one of her favorite words. Thinking was a good word, but analyzing was even better. She felt smarter when she used the word in class, and she was very pleased to use it in her essay about her winter vacation. Her teacher Mrs. Rapp even put a smiley face next to the word. Consuela was even more determined to learn all of the words on the lists. She even liked helping her little brother out with his words. School was starting to make sense.

What Makes Strategies Really Work

Marzano (2011) emphasizes that the success of intervention strategies has a lot to do with the level of teacher mastery. For example, effect sizes in one-to-one tutoring interventions have demonstrated increase by 48% (Bloom 1984), 16% (Erlbaum et al, 2000), and 12% (Ritter et al, 2009) in reading. Similarly, effect sizes in compare/contrast interventions have shown increases by 45% (Marzano, Pickering, & Pollock, 2001), 25% (Beele & Apthorp, 2010) and 18% (Haystead & Marzano, 2009).

Four Levels of Strategy Implementation

- *Beginning Level (Strategy mistakes are common & a lack of confidence)*
- *Developing Level (Decent levels of implementation & at ease with the strategy)*
- *Applying Level (Teacher & student confidence & effective teacher monitoring)*
- *Innovating Level (Teachers & students innovatively adapt the strategy to needs)*

The degree to which we and our students master strategies has a significant impact on the ultimate learning results. Remember that,

"A little bit every day is better than a lot in May."

We learn most new words incrementally, just by reading, a 10% average gain on a single reading. David Pearson says,

"The more they know, the better they understand
The better they understand, the more they learn
The more they learn, the more they know…"

As students advance through school the responsibility to gather information from reading textbooks becomes a much greater burden on students. Our students need to be able to identify textbooks structures to help them glean the important information continued within their pages.

Intervention Strategy #11: Identifying Text Structure

Our students as they enter middle school and high school spend more and more time interacting and negotiating meaning with textbooks (or more precisely the authors of textbooks.) Dickson, Simmons, and Kame'enui (1995) emphasize the importance of identifying text.

> *"Text structure refers to the organizational features that serve as a frame or pattern to guide and help readers identify important information and logical connections between ideas."*

The following suggestions can help students with informative textbooks.

Scaffolding Textbooks for Students

- *Preview Text Structure*
- *Preview Visuals*
- *Sequence*
- *Compare and Contrast*
- *Analyze Cause and Effect*
- *Identify Main Ideas*
- *Identify Supporting Evidence*
- *Create Outlines*

The great reading specialist David Pearson reminds us,

> *"Don't let reading remain America's curricular bully!"*

There are four basic types of text structures that authors use to organize and explain information. It is imperative that students explicitly understand these different types of text structures and can easily identify them.

Types of Informational Text Structures

- *Cause and Effect or Problem/Solution*

- *Compare/Contrast*

- *Description or Explanation*

- *Sequencing or Time-Order*

Students should know the four types of informational text structure and be able to explain them on a test. Just as inferring is critical to language comprehension, text structure is critical to literacy comprehension of large passages, and it ultimately contributes to effective learning. Carlisle and Rice (2002) share an important method for identifying text structure,

> *"Mayer used the term signaling to refer to various linguistic devices that a writer might use to help the reader follow the structure of a text. Because signaling helps the reader understand the organization of ideas, it affects both comprehension and recall."*

The following chart (adapted from Honig, et al., 2000) outlines several important text structures and the signal words that alert the reader to upcoming patterns for organizing information in the text:

Text Structure	Signal Words	Message to Reader
Cause/ Effect or Problem/Solution	*Because, due to, since, therefore, so as a result, consequently, nonetheless, if…then, accordingly, thus, nevertheless*	These signal words alert the reader to cause(s) leading to effect(s) or problem(s) leading to solutions.

Compare and Contrast	*Like, just as, similar, both, also, too, unlike, different, but, in contrast, on the other hand, although, yet, either...or, however, while, as well as, not only...but also, comparatively, likewise, instead*	The signal words alert the reader to upcoming comparisons and contrasts
Description or Explanation	*moreover, as with most, additionally, in other words, furthermore, second, next, then, finally, most important, also, in fact, significantly, imagine that, for instance, particularly, for example, in front, beside, near,*	The signal words alert the reader to an upcoming list or set of characteristics.
Sequencing or Time-Order	*Before, eventually, first, during, while as, frequently, at the same time, after, initially, whenever, secondly, then, next, at last, finally, now, recently, when, to begin with*	The signal words alert the reader to a sequence of events, actions or steps.

The following steps will help students learn various text structures as they read content-area information (adapted from Readance, Bean, & Baldwin, 2004).

Text Structure Steps

1. **Explain the types of text structure patterns** *and provide a simple example of each type*
2. **Invite readers to brainstorm their own list** *of potential transition signal words which can provide clues to text structure patterns*
3. **Ask your students to look for examples** *in their textbook of those patterns*
4. **Have students discuss why** *different material was organized by the author in a particular text pattern*
5. **Encourage your students to use signal words** *to recognize text structure patterns*

As students learn to recognize the academic language words that signal these common text structures and the patterns used to organize concepts, then they will be able to make better connections with the core content contained in the text. Various text structures use different academic language words to signal their presence. Academic language provides important signals for informing the reader of the type of organizational or syntactical structure used by the author. Textbooks that are constructed using text structures are easier to read, understand, and remember.

Creating Knowledge Structures

When we bridge the gap between two concepts by understanding how they relate to one another and how they are connected, then create a chunk of knowledge. This chunk of knowledge or data can then be connected to other chunks of knowledge to create patterns. Processing chunks and holding them in our working memory. Our working memory has quantitative limits. Our working memory is taxed by the amount of information that can fit in it and it is taxed by the amount of time that it can hold the information and process this information. When a conceptual pattern is thoroughly understood then this pattern takes up the cognitive space of a chunk. The reciprocal relationship between word knowledge and comprehension means an improvement in reading comprehension, in turn, increases a students' ability to learn more words and academic terminology and visa-versa. The decoding process of "learning to read" also needs the inferring process of "reading to learn." Effective teachers seem to innately understand the importance of helping students negotiate their learning gaps by helping them learn how to more successfully make inferences. As students improve their ability to see the organization of written text and the author's intent for writing, then the reader will be able to better recognize the purposes behind their reading and make meaning for the text. Moats (2000) notes that,

"Comprehension depends, firstly, on a large, working vocabulary and substantial background knowledge."

Making meaning is actually enhanced by communicating at a pace which allows the listener or reader to make inferences and piece the story or information together without requiring redundant statements to connect every concept. Part of the beauty of rich descriptive language is its ability to express many simultaneous ideas which encourage readers or listeners to make a multitude of inferences. Language is the medium or method in which we convey conceptual knowledge. As we understand how language is organized, it will help us better understand how knowledge is organized.

Comparing the Functions of our Conversations

Casual/Social Functions	*Academic Language Functions*
Greet someone	*Retell the story*
Answer simple questions	*Describe how a character is feeling*
Ask simple questions	*Compare and contrast two plots*
Respond to commands	*Analyze an author's intent*
Describe how one is feeling	*Infer what else a character might do*
Share an exciting event	*Question one's own reading of a text*
Communicate with adults	*Predict what might occur in a story*
Get along with peers	*Use background knowledge*
Work on a project with others	*Create a play or readers theater*
Play a game with friends	*Support one's own opinion*

Chat on the playground	*Participate in a role play*
Share a snack or lunch	*Interact in the science center*
Chat with the lunch lady	*Negotiate with a partner on a project*
Acknowledge others ideas	*Read a math word problem*
Disagree politely	*Summarize the plot of a story*
Offer a suggestion	*Describe a genre*
Solicit a response	*Share a news article*
Report a group's idea	*Write a hypothesis for science*
Agree politely	*Work on a social studies investigation*
Report partner's idea	*Synthesize information from two texts*
Ask for clarification	*Ask questions of an author's intentions*

Developing comprehension is built upon reciprocal relationships. For example strengthening fluency improves comprehension, and improving comprehension strengthens fluency. Acquiring academic language improves comprehension, and improving comprehension develops one's ability to acquire more academic language. Students who enter school with gaps in their language lack the ability to identify terms and key concepts that will help them learn effectively and efficiently at school. These students need explicit instruction. Understanding this synergistic relationship between academic language and academic literacy is vital to improving every student's academic success. Academic language is learned in academic settings through explicit instruction and through structured activities that scaffold and support learning. Research shows that gaps in literacy and learning can be overcome, if students receive instruction in academic language that is both explicit and systematic.

Academic Literacy and Reading

Researchers have determined that reading is a method by which only approximately 10-15% of the material is retained for specific recall and specific use. At the same time research also shows that reading a variety of texts and many pages a year is the number one indicator of learners who progress in academic language, content language, and concept knowledge. The key to reading may be that specific short term recall may see limited results, yet the long term general understanding of background knowledge may be strengthened and expanded. So in the long term One of the worst things an instructor can do is lecture for twenty or thirty minutes straight and then assign the class to read out of the textbook or complete some worksheet manufactured by the textbook publishers. Research shows that this is the least effective method for providing instruction to any learner, and English language learners and students of poverty particularly struggle with this approach.

Academic language is essential in helping students transition from decoding (learning to read) to comprehension (reading to learn).

Students from poverty, English Language Learners, and struggling readers all have difficulty accessing learning, because they lack the background knowledge and essential language that leads to effective learning.

Intervention Strategy #12: Academic Talk

Speaking and listening are also important abilities that constitute a literate person in our increasingly competitive world. Communicating ideas efficiently and actively listening to others. Speaking and listening are important in working as a team member in a collaborative fashion with others. Speaking and listening helps students develop the communication patterns that are part of different professional discourse. In addition to communicating actively with others, students will benefit from their abilities to view graphs, charts, recognize patterns, and organize data graphically. Speaking and listening are also important abilities that constitute a literate person in our increasingly competitive world. Taylor and Pearson (2006) summarize the research and note that,

"In low income schools, the amount of high level talk about text, challenging assignments, student-centered instruction, and high levels of student engagement predicts growth in student achievement on a variety of measures."

Communicating ideas efficiently and actively listening to others. Speaking and listening are important in working as a team member in a collaborative fashion with others. Speaking and listening helps students develop the communication patterns that are part of different professional discourse.

Picture: Two girls engage in academic talk about text.

In addition to communicating actively with others, students will benefit from their abilities to view graphs, charts, recognize patterns, and organize data graphically. Building a foundation and framework for students, particularly English language learners, and others who may be several grade levels behind their peers is crucial in bridging the achievement gap. Terms like analysis, interpretation, investigation can be used in each of the core content areas. Creating advanced academic literacy through language skills, key concepts, and powerful patterns is a process that continues over a lifetime for learners (Alexander, 2007). Academic talk is structured talk which extends and expands student understanding. Wolfram et al. (1999) note that,

"Meanings are usually made more fully explicit through words in academic talk. Language may also have different functions in academic interaction than in family or community interaction."

As we deliver academic instruction that scaffolds academic talk our classroom conversations will become much richer, and we will develop more in-depth understanding for our students.

Academic Talk Strategies

- *Tapping Prior Knowledge*
- *Predicting*
- *Picturing*
- *Internal Questioning*
- *Making Connections*
- *Generalizing*
- *Forming Interpretations*
- *Clarifying Issues*
- *Relating our Learning*
- *Reflecting on our Learning*

Students should engage in academic talk in class in all of the content areas. The following academic talk sentence frames adapted from (Johnson, 2009) provide a scaffold for students as they engage in academic talk in various content areas.

Tapping Prior Knowledge:

- ❖ *I already know that...*
- ❖ *This reminds me of...*
- ❖ *This relates to...*

Predicting

- ❖ *I guess that . . .*
- ❖ *Based on . . ., I predict that . . .*
- ❖ *I hypothesize that . .*

Picturing

- ❖ *I can see . . .*
- ❖ *I can imagine . . .*
- ❖ *I can visualize . . .*

Internal Questioning

- ❖ *How does this fit together . . .*
- ❖ *I wonder about . . .*
- ❖ *Could this mean . . .*

Asking Questions of Others

- ❖ *I wonder why . . .*
- ❖ *What if we . . .*
- ❖ *How is it possible that . . .*

Making Connections

- ❖ *This is like . . .*
- ❖ *This reminds me of . . .*
- ❖ *This looks like a pattern . . .*

Generalizing

- ❖ *So the big idea is . . .*
- ❖ *The conclusion I am drawing . . .*
- ❖ *The general impact is . . .*

Clarifying Issues

- ❖ *I'm confused about . . .*
- ❖ *I'm still unclear about . . .*
- ❖ *Can you explain more about . . .*

Forming Interpretations:

- ❖ *What this means to me is . . .*
- ❖ *I think this represents . . .*
- ❖ *The idea I'm getting is . . .*

Relating our learning

- ❖ *This is relevant because . . .*
- ❖ *This concept relates to . . .*
- ❖ *As I learned about . . .*

Reflecting on learning

- ❖ *The most important concept I learned today was . . .*
- ❖ *My favorite comment from a classmate was . . .*
- ❖ *The most challenging part of our activity was . . .*

Academic talk is intended to extend, to clarify, to state exceptions, to give examples, to make connections, and amplify understanding and more within targeted content area discussions.

Academic Language supports Professional Discourse

Professions use the abstract action language of academic language. In these professions they analyze, synthesize, write detailed reports, and interact in formal contexts. When a student comes home and asks for help from a parent who knows and lives the language of their profession, the parents can give help and support. They can easily explain in detail, give examples of ways to approach the question, provide partial answers and let their student fill in the rest, give analogies etc. Now an engineer may try to compare analysis in language arts to analysis in aircraft design, yet the parents are capable of giving the support. They faced these questions in high school and most of them faced these questions in college where their major course of discipline may have been very different, yet they took the necessary pre-requisites to have a broad education. This academic language is tied to specific terminology and higher you go in school the more specific the academic language becomes. For example to a kid the skeletal parts that keep a body together are commonly known as bones. To an aspiring doctor in medical school, each bone has a name and various properties that make it unique to the proper functioning of the human body. As students become better at identifying the different types of academic language they will be better prepared to access grade level text and succeed in school.

Reflection Questions
1) *What was your favorite concept and favorite strategy that you learned so far in the book?*
2) *How are you going to make sure RTI strategies are effectively implemented throughout your school?*

Chapter Five:
RTI Principles
for Learning

*"Leadership and Learning are
Indispensable to each other"*

John F. Kennedy

Natalie found out that she was struggling in school when her teacher told her mother, "I think Natalie is faking kindergarten." Natalie's mother was understandably upset. Who fakes kindergarten? Natalie was a bright, engaging five year-old who loved school. What a crazy thing for Natalie's teacher to say that she was faking kindergarten. The comment seemed to be forgotten as that summer Natalie and her family moved to the other side of the country and she enrolled in a new school. Natalie struggled a bit in First Grade, yet it was only a little bit and anyways she truly enjoyed school. It wasn't until the beginning of second grade that a vision screening discovered that Natalie needed glasses, and fact she needed a very thick prescription. Her eyesight was dismal, so it seems that Natalie, who played well with others, was often placed in the back of the room far away from a chalk board that she could not see. It appeared Natalie's kindergarten teacher was right that she was faking her ability to read the whiteboard and learn. Now that Natalie had glasses, it seemed it would just be a matter of time before she was able to catch up with her peers. Instead, she continued to struggle as she entered third grade. Her third grade teacher would get frustrated when Natalie would begin work, yet she would quickly melt and stop working about 15 minutes later. It took a lot of testing and time to discover that Natalie also had Attention Deficit Disorder (ADD). By fifth grade she had medicine and it seemed she should be getting back on track, yet Natalie got further and further behind her peers. It wasn't until seventh grade that further testing discovered that Natalie also had visual tracking issues, where her eyes were unable to follow the words on the page. Like dyslexia, the visual tracking causes words and sentences to become scrambled and extremely difficult to read. Finally in the tenth grade, Natalie was able to catch up to her peers and read at grade level. It seems that staring out the window and neglecting to read the whiteboard had stunted Natalie's ability to read, pay attention, visually track words, and learn at an effective rate. Natalie is a challenged reader.

What Makes Strategies Really Work

All of the strategies that have been covered in this book have been designed to expand your repertoire of instructional tools. As our instruction improves, student learning will improve. The NEA (2006) outlines the role of General Education Teachers in the RTI Process

> RtI is *"the practice of providing high quality instruction and intervention matched to student skill needs, monitoring student progress frequently to make changes in instructional goals, and applying child response data to important educational decisions."*

As we add more tools to our instructional toolbox, then we will be able to reach more students and achieve greater academic results. Most teachers only use a handful of strategies and it is important that we embrace a variety of strategies to meet the increasing needs of our students. Now let's take a moment to reflect on how Intervention support is provided to our students. Take some time and answer the following questions in the Response to Intervention – RTI Survey.

<u>Response to Intervention - RTI Survey</u>

1. **What does your school do for your Struggling Readers?**

    _____

    _____

2. **How does your school organize Tier I RTI instruction?**

    _____

    _____

3. **How does you school organize Tier II RTI instruction?**

    _____

    _____

4. **How does your school organize Tier III RTI instruction?**

    _____

    _____

5. **What does your school do for your English Learners?**

    _____

    _____

6. **What does your school do for your Special Needs Students?**

    _____

    _____

7. **What assessments does your school use for your RTI Students?**

    _____

    _____

8. **How often does your school assess your student's progress?**

    _____

    _____

9. **What does your school do to support Tier I RTI students?**

    _____

    _____

10. **What does your school do to support Tier II RTI students?**

    _____

    _____

11. **What does your school do to support Tier III RTI students?**

    _____

    _____

12. **How often does your school meet to look over RTI student's progress?**

_____

_____

The survey can help inform our personal and school-wide understanding for developing an RTI program. Now let's ask an important question. Why should we implement RTI in our schools?

- Because it outlines a **Coordinated system** of service delivery that focuses on meeting the Instructional needs of all students
- Emphasis of RTI is **all about prevention**
- RTI in the classroom and school is **"not a wait to fail"** model
- Focuses on **working as a TEAM** to meet the needs of students
- Provides an **instructional match** for students with evidence-based
- practices and interventions
- Encourages **Data-based decision making** that takes place in teams
- — Provides effective support for **low socio-economic** students, struggling readers, and **English learners**.

There is also a legal rationale for implementing RTI in our classrooms and schools.

Legal Rationale for implementing an RTI framework.

- *No Child Left Behind (NCLB)*
- *Individuals with Disabilities Education Improvement Act (IDEA)*
- *State mandates*

An effective RTI program includes three key components: Screening, Instructional Tiered Support, and Monitoring. It is important to survey all students by screening them and getting a baseline understanding of their general needs. Next, and most important, we need to provide tiered instructional support that is targeted to the needs of the students. And finally, we need to monitor our student's progress. Let's now look at each of these components:

① Screening

- All students are assessed at the beginning of the school year
- Identify students that are most in need of extra instructional support

② Instructional Tiered Support

- Tiered support and intervention to meet individual student needs
- Support is provided as early as kindergarten.

③ Progress Monitoring

- Assess and Track the progress of students struggling to achieve grade level skills, concepts, and processes at least 3 times per year.
- Determine the interventions effects and when instructional change is needed.

Most schools already address each principle in some way. RTI is about improving and streamlining screening, instructional, and monitoring processes so that we can make accurate data-based decisions. While screening helps us identify those students who need the most time and attention to improve their learning abilities, the key to improving RTI results is to apply effective research-based strategies. Consider the following:

- **Education will improve as fast as our instructional Leadership improves**
- **Instruction = Internal + Structures**
- **Interventions should focus on Instruction instead of Restructuring**

In education, we have spent countless amounts of time, dollars, and resources over the years on restructuring our schools, when we really need to be focusing on improving instruction. The following chart outlines many of the key components of an effectively three-tiered RTI support system.

	Tier I	Tier 2	Tier 3
Time	30 min. in K-6 5 min. per class	60 – 90 min. 30 – 60 min.	90 – 120 min. 60 – 120 min.
Method	Classroom Small-Group Instruction (4-6)	Targeted Push-In or Pull-Out (2-6)	Intensive Specialist Suppport (1-2)
Areas of Focus	5 areas	2-4 areas	1-2 areas
Progress Monitoring Assessment	Assess 3 times a year by Teacher &Daily Observation	Assessments by Specialists & Chart Weekly Progress	Assessments by Psychologist & Chart Daily Progress

As our students are provided consistent screening, effective instructional strategies, and follow-up progress monitoring, they will begin to see tangible results that will build their confidence as learners. As your entire class increases their desire and ability to learn and interact with language and literacy the culture of your classroom will improve. Let's now review some of the key benefits of implementing RTI strategies in the classroom.

What benefits do Intervention Strategies Provide?

- **Easy to implement** (e.g., time during class/prep time)
- **Highly effective Evidence-based**(i.e., Engaging, Provide Access, Make Meaning)

- **Strategies are scaffolded or structured**
- **Para-educators can implement in small groups**

As we provide our students with effective support with improved instructional strategies that give students more time and more attention where they need it most, we will start to see significant improvements in student learning and academic results. Let's now look at a few statements that we may often hear at school regarding how our students are doing academically.

What do we often hear about struggling students?

❖ *"Juan is having a hard time reading."*
❖ *"Maria is below grade-level."*
❖ *"Sarah doesn't pay attention during science block."*
❖ *"Larry is unmotivated and has poor behavior."*

What's lacking in these descriptions? The statements lack the specific information that can come from classroom-wide or school-wide screening that is followed with targeted progress monitoring. We need to do a better job of specifically targeting student's needs, so that we can provide the most appropriate classroom interventions. The more targeted ours assessments are, then the more targeted we can be with our instructional interventions. Let's now look at screening and progress monitoring in more detail

SCREENING is the process of administering an assessment to all students in a population (grade, school) to allocate instructional resources

- Allows us to determine instructional needs, or give students access to the instructional strategies that meet their needs
- Done 3 times per year (fall, winter, spring)
- Data is discussed in grade level teams (PLC's) to allocate resources
- Example: Which students need extra help in phonics?

PROGRESS MONITORING is the frequent and repeated collection of student data over a period of time

- Ongoing assessment on a daily or weekly basis
- Linked to GAINS in student achievement and changes in teachers' instruction
- Allows us to evaluate interventions or programs based on several data points, rather than one or two, or anecdotal descriptions
- Research indicates 6 or more data points are needed to get accurate monitoring
- Example: Is peer tutoring helping Johnny increase his oral reading fluency?

After screening all students, here are a few thoughts on designing an effective progress monitoring plan to follow-up with students who still struggle in language, literacy, and learning.

<u>**Designing a Progress Monitoring Plan**</u>

1. Describe the student's current level of performance (baseline)

2. Select assessment tool that identifies learning needs

3. Develop a Learning Goal

4. Implement Intervention Strategies

5. Chart Data Points and Adjust Instruction

While RTI began in Iowa many of the assessment resources have been developed at the University of Oregon as part of what is called Dynamic Indicators of Early Literacy Skills or DIBELS. These assessment tools can be used for comprehensive screening and for targeted progress monitoring. Here are a few of the assessment tools provided on the DIBELS website.

Table 1.1 Alignment of *DIBELS Next* Measures with Basic Early Literacy Skills

Basic Early Literacy Skills	*DIBELS* Indicators
Phonemic Awareness	First Sound Fluency (FSF) Phoneme Segmentation Fluency (PSF)
Alphabetic Principle and Basic Phonics	Nonsense Word Fluency (NWF) –Correct Letter Sounds –Whole Words Read
Advanced Phonics and Word Attack Skills	*DIBELS* Oral Reading Fluency (DORF) –Accuracy
Accurate and Fluent Reading of Connected Text	*DIBELS* Oral Reading Fluency (DORF) –Correct Words Per Minute –Accuracy
Reading Comprehension	Daze *DIBELS* Oral Reading Fluency (DORF) –Correct Words Per Minute –Retell Total/Quality of Response
Vocabulary and Language Skills	Word Use Fluency-Revised (WUF-R)(available as an experimental measure from http://dibels.org/)

In addition to the DIBELS or AimsWEB resources, the following RTI resources can also help in supporting your RTI program.

Additional RTI Resources

- *What Works Clearinghouse*(intervention effectiveness information and more intervention options) http://ies.ed.gov/ncee/wwc/
- *Florida Center for Reading Research* (interventions and effectiveness information)http://www.fcrr.org/
- *Developmental Studies Center*
- *Center On Instruction* High School Specific Information http://www.centeroninstruction.org/topic.cfm?s=1&k=R&c=34

The preceding RTI resources provide additional research and ideas for implementing a response to intervention program effectively. Before we conclude this chapter on RTI strategies, let's squeeze in one more strategy that can help in grades Kindergarten through third.

Bonus Intervention Strategy: Fluency Phones

Young students (grades one through three) love to use fluency phones. They are inexpensive and easy to make. Each fluency phone can be made from part sound at the local hardware store plumbing aisle. They cost about $2.97 cents to make one. The reading lists can be obtained by going to the University of Oregon's Dibels website at https://dibels.uoregon.edu/measures/. Consider the following ideas when using fluency phones in the classroom.

Fluency Phones

1. *Students in K-2 and any student that is behind in grades 3 or above will benefit from fluency phones.*
2. *In 2nd grade use fluency phones for 5-10 minutes a day.*
3. *Students should grab their bag with their phone and their reading passages.*
4. *Students should read and practice out loud their pronunciation and their fluency.*
5. *The teacher should quickly monitor students and then get started on small group instruction.*

Fluency phones are engaging, help structure reading tasks, provide students access, and help create meaning. Fluency phones work best when they reading opportunities are provided on a consistent daily basis.

Summary

Designing and implementing an RTI framework in your school needs to have an effective structure with consistent screening and progress monitoring. Yet, the most important factor in creating a successful RTI program is to provide effective classroom strategies that prevent students from falling behind and help bridge the gaps students may have in their learning. I hope that as you apply the strategies that we have covered, you will have fun with your students and help them achieve academically. Please share these strategies with your colleagues so that all of our students can benefit in ways that will make the students at your school more confident learners. As we wrap-up the strategies chapters of this book, enjoy the grade level academic language lists and academic vocabulary lists that have been specifically designed for each grade level.

Reflection Questions

1. *How do I monitor the progress my students are achieving when I implement the strategies covered in the previous chapters?*
2. *How can I make sure that I use all of the strategies that are appropriate for my grade level with my students?*

Notes

Chapter Six:

Kindergarten Academic Language & Academic Vocabulary

"Once you learn to read,
you will be forever free."

Frederick Douglass

As children enter school they come with sizable differences in the amount of vocabulary they know. Students from low socio-economic backgrounds typically have half of the words in their vocabulary compared to their higher socio-economic peers. This gap exists as early as age three. While the students typically have similar cognitive abilities, the difference in vocabulary knowledge can dramatically impact the rate at which kinders can learn new knowledge. It is important to teach explicitly those words that will help students overcome this disparity in word knowledge. The upcoming chapters outline the essential academic mortar words and academic brick words which will help student academically succeed for their grade level. Each chapter contains **75 general academic language** (mortar) words (Johnson, 2009), **75 social science academic vocabulary** (brick) words, **75 mathematics academic vocabulary** (brick) words, **50 science academic vocabulary** (brick) words, and **50 language arts academic vocabulary** (brick) words. Make sure that each student understands these words and can readily define them.

Kindergarten (Mortar) Johnson Academic Language List

1.	Act	39.	Link
2.	Add	40.	List
3.	After	41.	Listen
4.	Aid	42.	Make
5.	Always	43.	Minus
6.	Answer	44.	Never
7.	Apply	45.	Order
8.	Ask	46.	Plus
9.	Before	47.	Prepare
10.	Build	48.	Print
11.	But	49.	Question
12.	Care	50.	Read
13.	Chart	51.	Role
14.	Choose	52.	Rule
15.	Collect	53.	Same
16.	Compare	54.	Save
17.	Decrease	55.	Say
18.	Differ	56.	Sense
19.	Equal	57.	Share
20.	Find	58.	Show
21.	Finish	59.	Speak
22.	Fix	60.	Subtract
23.	Focus	61.	Support
24.	Gather	62.	Task
25.	Get	63.	Team
26.	Give	64.	Tell
27.	Go	65.	Test
28.	Goal	66.	Think
29.	Group	67.	Understand
30.	Guess	68.	View
31.	Help	69.	What
32.	How	70.	When
33.	If	71.	Where
34.	Include	72.	Who
35.	Join	73.	Why
36.	Know	74.	Work
37.	Label	75.	Write
38.	Like		

Kindergarten Social Studies (Bricks) Academic Vocabulary List

1. Airplane
2. Alphabet
3. America
4. Apartment
5. Bicycle
6. Boat
7. Car
8. Celebration
9. Chief
10. City
11. Cloud
12. Cold
13. Community
14. Computer
15. Country
16. Dam
17. Desert
18. Direction
19. Earth
20. East
21. Fairness
22. Family
23. Flag
24. Forest
25. Future
26. Group
27. Harvest
28. Hill
29. History
30. Holiday
31. Hot
32. House
33. Human Being
34. Ice
35. Igloo
36. Island
37. Jungle
38. Language
39. Leader
40. Map
41. Mayor
42. Mining
43. Mountain
44. Needs
45. Neighborhood
46. North
47. Past
48. Peace
49. Pledge
50. Prairie
51. Present
52. President
53. Rain
54. Respect
55. River
56. Rules
57. Sea
58. Season
59. Seeds
60. Sheep herder
61. Snow
62. Soil
63. South
64. State
65. Temperature
66. Town
67. Transportation
68. Tribe
69. Valley
70. Village
71. Vote
72. Wants
73. Weather
74. West
75. Wind

Kindergarten Mathematics (Bricks) Academic Vocabulary List

1. Add
2. After
3. Before
4. Beginning
5. Below
6. Between
7. Bigger
8. Both
9. Bottom
10. Calendar
11. Center
12. Circle
13. Compare
14. Count
15. Day
16. Each
17. Eight
18. Eighteen
19. Eighty
20. Eleven (th)
21. End
22. Equal
23. Fifteen (th)
24. Fifty
25. Five (fth)
26. Forty
27. Four (th)
28. Fourteen (th)
29. Greater Than
30. Hundred
31. Larger
32. Last
33. Left
34. Less
35. Line
36. Mathematics
37. Middle
38. MinuS
39. Minute
40. Month
41. Nine
42. Nineteen (th)
43. Ninety
44. Number
45. One
46. Plus
47. Point
48. Rectangle
49. Right
50. Ruler
51. Seven (th)
52. Seventeen (th)
53. Seventy
54. Shape
55. Sign
56. Six
57. Sixteen (th)
58. Sixty
59. Smaller
60. Square
61. Ten
62. Thirteen (th)
63. Thirty
64. Three
65. Time
66. Top
67. Total
68. Triangle
69. Twelve (fth)
70. Twenty
71. Two
72. Unit
73. Week
74. Year
75. Zero

Kindergarten Science (Bricks) Academic Vocabulary List

1. Air	26. Moon
2. Animal	27. Mouth
3. Ant	28. Ocean
4. Beak	29. Power
5. Bird	30. Rain
6. Bones	31. Roots
7. Branch	32. Season
8. Breathe	33. Senses
9. Cloud	34. Sight
10. Clue	35. Skin
11. Cold	36. Slope
12. Dark	37. Smell
13. Dry	38. Sound
14. Ear	39. Speed
15. Earth	40. Spring
16. Echo	41. Stars
17. Equator	42. Summer
18. Fall	43. Sun
19. Fish	44. Swamp
20. Hail	45. Taste
21. Hair	46. Tongue
22. Hear	47. Touch
23. Hot	48. Warm
24. Leaf	49. Water
25. Light	50. Winter

Kindergarten Language Arts (Bricks) Academic Vocabulary List

1. Alphabet
2. Author
3. Beginning
4. Book
5. Capital
6. Consonant
7. Dictionary
8. Drawing
9. Ending
10. Exclamation mark
11. Fairy tale
12. Guess
13. Hear
14. How
15. Illustrator
16. Left to Right
17. Letter
18. Listen
19. Lower case
20. Middle
21. Period
22. Picture book
23. Pictures
24. Poem
25. Prediction
26. Print
27. Pronunciation
28. Question
29. Read
30. Retell
31. Rhyme
32. Sentence
33. Song
34. Sound
35. Sound-Letter relationship
36. Speak
37. Spelling
38. Story
39. Tell
40. Title
41. Understand
42. Uppercase case
43. Vowel
44. What
45. When
46. Where
47. Who
48. Why
49. Word
50. Write

Chapter Seven:

First Grade Academic Language
& Academic Vocabulary

"Children are like cement.
Whatever falls on them
makes an impression."
Dr. Haim Ginott

First grade students become aware of the world them and particularly words. As the first graders observe the world around them, they develop a much greater sense of word awareness or word consciousness. Suddenly the letters on stop signs take on greater meaning. S-T-O-P means something in addition to the red hexagon shape that causes cars to sop. Kids in first grade as we provide them the foundation of phonemic awareness and sounds begin to sound out words and recognize them in the world around them. When my son Benjamin was in the first grade he was so thrilled when he realized he could read the signs at McDonald's. As we were going through the drive-thru picking up a happy meal, Benjamin announced, "That sign says "Please have your money ready" and the next sign said, "Have a nice day!" He declared excitedly, "I can read." He was so anxious that evening to get out one of his books and read to me rather than have me read to him. It was amazing how quickly everything came together. Benjamin went from slowly sounding out words to comprehending complete sentences. We need to take advantage of this exciting new world of words and make sure that all students obtain the basic building blocks of content vocabulary and the mortar of academic language for their grade level.

1ˢᵗ Grade (Mortar) Johnson Academic Language List

1. Again
2. Aid
3. Almost
4. Another
5. Appreciate
6. Aware
7. Because
8. Check
9. Collect
10. Combine
11. Community
12. Contrast
13. Control
14. Cooperate
15. Define
16. Deliver
17. Describe
18. Different
19. Discuss
20. During
21. Earlier
22. Earn
23. Educate
24. Emotional
25. Encourage
26. Energy
27. Explain
28. Finally
29. Gather
30. Greet
31. Grow
32. Guide
33. Highlight
34. Hire
35. Idea
36. Identify
37. Infer
38. Instruct
39. Involve
40. Know
41. Language
42. Later
43. Learn
44. Locate
45. Meet
46. Memorize
47. Mental
48. Nearly
49. Next
50. Now
51. Part
52. Pattern
53. Physical
54. Place
55. Practice
56. Preview
57. Primary
58. Prior
59. Proceed
60. Progress
61. Rate
62. Recall
63. Report
64. Reverse
65. Review
66. Similar
67. Since
68. Soon
69. Study
70. Suggest
71. Target
72. Then
73. Unlike
74. Weigh
75. Yet

1st Grade Social Science (Bricks) Academic Vocabulary List

1. Africa
2. Air force
3. Antarctica
4. Area
5. Army
6. Artic
7. Asia
8. Atlantic
9. Australia
10. Bay
11. Carnival
12. City Hall
13. Cliff
14. Coast
15. Communication
16. Compass
17. Continent
18. Cooperation
19. Cotton
20. County
21. Dairy
22. Earthquake
23. Election
24. Europe
25. Explorer
26. Famine
27. Fruits
28. Geography
29. Gin
30. Globe
31. Governor
32. Guide
33. Hazy
34. Historian
35. Indian
36. Judge
37. Justice
38. Land
39. Landowner
40. Language
41. Law
42. Marines
43. Market
44. Mill
45. Mountain Range
46. Nature
47. Navy
48. Neighborhood
49. North America
50. North Pole
51. Oats
52. Ocean
53. Pacific
54. People
55. Planet
56. Potato
57. Property
58. Region
59. Responsibilities
60. Rice
61. Rights
62. Seashore
63. South America
64. South Pole
65. Statue
66. Stream
67. Swamp
68. Tide
69. Timeline
70. Tools
71. Train
72. Trap
73. Tropical
74. Vegetables
75. Wheat

1st Grade Mathematics (Bricks) Academic Vocabulary List

1. Above
2. Across
3. Addition
4. Alike
5. All
6. Altogether
7. Amount
8. Apart
9. Around
10. Base
11. Cent
12. Change
13. Clock
14. Close
15. Complete
16. Contain
17. Different
18. Digit
19. Dime
20. Dollar
21. Dozen
22. Empty
23. Even
24. Far
25. Feet
26. Few
27. First
28. Foot
29. Group
30. Half (lves)
31. Half-past
32. High (er)
33. Inch
34. Inequality
35. Inside
36. Less
37. Long (er)
38. Low (er)
39. Many
40. Match
41. Mile
42. Missing
43. Money
44. Month
45. More
46. Most
47. Much
48. Multiple
49. Near
50. Next
51. Nickel
52. Ninth
53. None
54. Odd
55. Order
56. Outside
57. Pair
58. Part
59. Part
60. Round
61. Second
62. Set
63. Short (er)
64. Side
65. Size
66. Some
67. Subtract
68. Sum
69. Symbol
70. Tenth
71. Than
72. Unequal
73. Whole
74. Width
75. Yard

1st Grade Science (Bricks) Academic Vocabulary List

1. Animal Tracks
2. Battery
3. Blood
4. Burn
5. Coal
6. Compass
7. Dairy
8. Dinosaurs
9. Egg
10. Electricity
11. Energy
12. Fat
13. Food Pyramid
14. Fresh Water
15. Fruits
16. Funnel
17. Gas
18. Heat
19. Height
20. Investigation
21. Length
22. Liquid
23. Man-made
24. Measure
25. Meat
26. Moss
27. Muscles
28. Natural
29. Observe
30. Planets
31. Recycle
32. Reflect
33. Reptile
34. Salt Water
35. Skeleton
36. Smog
37. Soil
38. Solid
39. Steam
40. Temperature
41. Thermometer
42. Trunk
43. Valley
44. Vegetables
45. Vitamin
46. Wave
47. Weight
48. Wetlands
49. Wildlife
50. Wingspan

1ˢᵗ Grade Language Arts (Bricks) Academic Vocabulary List

1. Abbreviation
2. Accent
3. Blending
4. Capitalization
5. Chapter
6. Character
7. Choral Reading
8. Comma
9. Compound word
10. Comprehend
11. Consonant
12. Decode
13. Dictionary
14. Discussion
15. Fantasy
16. Fiction
17. Film
18. Hero
19. Heroine
20. Illustrations
21. Information
22. Media
23. Message
24. Myth
25. Nonfiction
26. Noun
27. Paragraph
28. Phonemic Awareness
29. Phonics
30. Poem
31. Predict
32. Question Mark
33. Reality
34. Response
35. Segmenting
36. Sequence
37. Setting
38. Speech
39. Standards
40. Statement
41. Story Map
42. Summarize
43. Syllable
44. Text
45. Topic
46. Verb
47. Video
48. Vocabulary
49. Vowel sound
50. Word Recognition

Chapter Eight:

Second Grade Academic Language & Academic Vocabulary

*"I may forget my first crush in second grade
but never my favorite teacher."*
Fehl Dungo

As students enter second grade their awareness of words is quickly expanding and they begin to recognize and read entire sentences. Most students can read at this age and the question becomes how fluently they can decode and process the words and information. It is important that students understand the relationships between letters and words, as well as words and sentences. By this grade students should develop mastery of all 43 sounds and recognize the sound-letter relationships. Students should also be able to make the connections regarding word-definition or word-picture relationships. When students see a particular word an image or picture that represents that word should pop into student's heads. For example, the word C-A-T should have a picture that represents it. Whether it is a little kitty, a tough alley cat, a fluffy calico, or sleek Siamese, students should begin to develop a picture as they read word the word CAT, and the pictures in their mind should take on movement and color as they read full sentences. The Fluency Phones strategy is a great strategy to give students classroom practice in reading and to make sure they are producing and understanding all 43 sounds in the English language. As second graders more fully develop their awareness of words and particularly the mortar words they will become more capable readers.

2nd Grade (Mortar) Johnson Academic Language List

1. Accept
2. Adapt
3. Almost
4. Also
5. Another
6. Arrange
7. Assess
8. Assign
9. Attract
10. Author
11. Balance
12. Behave
13. Beyond
14. Categorize
15. Chapter
16. Compare
17. Compete
18. Complete
19. Connect
20. Consider
21. Control
22. Cooperate
23. Crack
24. Design
25. Direct
26. Discipline
27. Edit
28. Educate
29. Encourage
30. Environment
31. Expert
32. External
33. Finally
34. Follow
35. Formula
36. General
37. Government
38. Inquire
39. Internal
40. Judge
41. Maybe
42. Measure
43. Nature
44. Negative
45. Neutral
46. Norm
47. Nurture
48. Objective
49. Occupation
50. Opinion
51. Option
52. Outcome
53. Participate
54. Persist
55. Positive
56. Possible
57. Power
58. Present
59. Probably
60. Proceed
61. Process
62. Purpose
63. Resource
64. Responsibility
65. Scan
66. Secondary
67. Select
68. Set up
69. So
70. Social
71. Summarize
72. Support
73. Target
74. Topic
75. Unity

2nd Grade Social Science (Bricks) Academic Vocabulary List

1. Arctic
2. Arctic
3. Art
4. Authority
5. Basic Needs
6. Boundary
7. Business
8. Canada
9. Citizen
10. Clan
11. Colorado River
12. Columbia River
13. Competition
14. Conflict
15. Continent
16. Cowboy
17. Creek
18. Custom
19. Decade
20. Drought
21. Duty
22. Education
23. Equator
24. Factory
25. Fertilizer
26. Fort
27. Fossil
28. Gender
29. Grasslands
30. Great Lakes
31. Gulf of Mexico
32. Harbor
33. Hemisphere
34. Humid
35. Independence
36. Invention
37. Irrigation
38. Landmark
39. Legal
40. Livestock
41. Manager
42. Mexico
43. Mississippi River
44. Model
45. Nation
46. Native American
47. Natural Resources
48. Patriotic
49. Pioneer
50. Pollution
51. Port
52. Primary
53. Produce
54. Railroad
55. Rio Grande
56. Role
57. Secondary
58. Servant
59. Settlement
60. Slave
61. Solar
62. Starvation
63. State Capital
64. Steel
65. Tax
66. Temple
67. Trade
68. Traffic
69. Travel
70. United States
71. Values
72. Volcano
73. Warehouse
74. Wealth
75. Weapons

Academic Language & Academic Vocabulary

2nd Grade Mathematics (Bricks) Academic Vocabulary List

1. Angle
2. Arabic Numerals
3. Area
4. Associative
5. Base Ten
6. Boundary
7. Cardinal Number
8. Centimeter
9. Commutative
10. Connect
11. Cost
12. Curve
13. Diagonal
14. Difference
15. Distance
16. Distributive
17. Double
18. Fact
19. Far
20. Fast
21. Figure
22. From
23. Gallon
24. Height
25. Inside
26. Join
27. Law
28. Length
29. Location
30. Measure
31. Member
32. Meter (ric)
33. Midpoint
34. Million
35. Model
36. Multiply
37. Near
38. Negative
39. Once
40. Opposite
41. Ounce
42. Outside
43. Over
44. Pint
45. Place value
46. Position
47. Positive
48. Pound
49. Product
50. Property
51. Quart
52. Quarter
53. Regroup
54. Repeat
55. Replace
56. Roman numerals
57. Row
58. Rule
59. Same
60. Score
61. Section
62. Series
63. Similar
64. Single
65. Take Away
66. Thick
67. Thin
68. Thousand
69. Thrice
70. Times
71. Triple
72. Twice
73. Under
74. Value
75. Weigh (t)

2nd Grade Science (Bricks) Academic Vocabulary List

1. Action
2. Axis
3. Backbone
4. Bacteria
5. Balance
6. Behavior
7. Cartilage
8. Change
9. Circulation
10. Cocoon
11. Contagious
12. Crater
13. Crystal
14. Data
15. Degrees
16. Disease
17. Distance
18. Divide
19. Earth's Rotation
20. Elevation
21. Environment
22. Exercise
23. Experiment
24. Flood
25. Fuel
26. Gasoline
27. Hurricane
28. Laboratory
29. Magnet
30. Mammal
31. Mineral
32. Mold
33. Ore
34. Population
35. Prediction
36. Process
37. Reaction
38. Revolve
39. Rotation
40. Sanitary
41. Scale
42. Scar
43. Section
44. Species
45. Spinal Cord
46. Tidal Wave
47. Tornado
48. Unit
49. Vapor
50. Wet

2ⁿᵈ Grade Language Arts (Bricks) Academic Vocabulary List

1. Adjective
2. Adverb
3. Antonyms
4. Apostrophe
5. Atlas
6. Audience
7. Author's purpose
8. Background Knowledge
9. Brainstorm
10. Cause
11. Character
12. Details
13. Draft
14. Edit
15. Effect
16. Encyclopedia
17. Encyclopedia
18. Fables
19. Fact
20. Fluency
21. Folktale
22. Glossary
23. Internet
24. Main idea
25. Multiple-meaning words
26. Narrative
27. Opinion
28. Organization
29. Phonological
30. Plot
31. Plural
32. Plural
33. Prediction
34. Prewrite
35. Pronoun
36. Publish
37. Quotation Marks
38. Read Aloud
39. Scan
40. Sentence fragment
41. Sequential
42. Setting
43. Singular
44. Singular
45. Skim
46. Stress
47. Synonyms
48. Table of contents
49. Word Awareness
50. Word Sort

Chapter Nine:

Third Grade Academic Language

& Academic Vocabulary

*"The greatest sign of success for
a teacher...is to be able to say,
The children are now working
as if I did not exist."*

Maria Montessori

Most third graders can usually decode fairly effectively. The challenge for so many at this age is whether or not they can comprehend effectively what they are decoding. While it is important that third graders read rapidly and that they can pronounce words properly and decode accurately, there is one more important aspect to fluency that is often over-looked. The third aspect of fluency is called prosody. The word prosody comes from the root word prose and it can be defined as the inflection, tone, and expression used when reads out loud. For example, someone quoting a soliloquy by Shakespeare out loud would want to use plenty of prosody. Fluency needs prosody in order to effectively develop comprehension. Third graders who decode rapidly and accurately, but read the words very flatly or without much expression lack prosody. These students need to fully understand the word definition or meaning of the word and then they will give the word the proper inflection, tone, and expression to convey the meaning. Listening to students read out loud is one way to determine if they are using prosody effectively and fully comprehending the words and passages they read. Third graders should be able to read all of the words on the third grade academic language list with prosody.

3rd Grade (Mortar) Johnson Academic Language List

1. Academic
2. Achieve
3. As
4. Assemble
5. Assess
6. Attitude
7. Attribute
8. Award
9. Balance
10. Believe
11. Bias
12. Chart
13. Clarify
14. Code
15. Communicate
16. Concept
17. Confidence
18. Control
19. Core
20. Cycle
21. Data
22. Decision
23. Demonstrate
24. Despite
25. Detect
26. Elect
27. Emotional
28. Employ
29. Eventually
30. Exercise
31. Experiment
32. Explore
33. Foundation
34. Frequently
35. Global
36. Grant
37. Immediately
38. Instead
39. Integrate
40. Intelligence
41. Introduce
42. Invite
43. Level
44. Mental
45. Method
46. Model
47. Objectives
48. Organize
49. Perhaps
50. Phase
51. Portfolio
52. Primary
53. Profession
54. Project
55. Publish
56. Punish
57. Quality
58. Quantity
59. Reflect
60. Region
61. Report
62. Self-control
63. Settle
64. Sketch
65. Social
66. Source
67. Supply
68. System
69. Theme
70. Train
71. Transport
72. Trend
73. Tutor
74. Until
75. While

3rd Grade Social Science (Bricks) Academic Vocabulary List

1. Aborigines
2. Apprentice
3. Arctic
4. Artifact
5. Assembly
6. Automatic
7. Barbarian
8. Barter
9. Bazaar
10. Blacksmith
11. Borders
12. Canyon
13. Chronology
14. City Council
15. Common
16. Consumer
17. Contribution
18. Court
19. Crime
20. Crops
21. Delta
22. Distance
23. Elect
24. Environment
25. Ethnic
26. Exports
27. Freedom
28. Frontier
29. Global
30. Immigrant
31. Imports
32. Interview
33. Iron Ore
34. Machete
35. Mainland
36. Map Key
37. Metropolitan
38. Migrate
39. Moisture
40. Nationality
41. Native
42. Nomad
43. Oasis
44. Paddy
45. Peninsula
46. Plain
47. Plantation
48. Plateau
49. Polar
50. Population
51. Privileges
52. Producer
53. Profit
54. Public
55. Pyramids
56. Region
57. Religion
58. Route
59. Rural
60. Service
61. Settlement
62. Sharecropper
63. Slum
64. Suburb
65. Technology
66. Telegraph
67. Territories
68. Thresh
69. Tradition
70. Unity
71. Urban
72. Veteran
73. Wages
74. Wholesale
75. Zone

3rd Grade Mathematics (Bricks) Academic Vocabulary List

1. Approximate
2. Braces
3. Celsius
4. Collection
5. Column
6. Combination
7. Common
8. Compute
9. Cone
10. Coordinates
11. Cube
12. Cylinder
13. Decimal
14. Diameter
15. Divide
16. Dividend
17. Divisible
18. Division
19. Divisor
20. Equivalent
21. Expand
22. Factor
23. Fahrenheit
24. Fraction (al)
25. Gallon
26. Graph
27. Graph
28. Grouping
29. Guess
30. Hexagon
31. Horizontal
32. Inquiry
33. Instead of
34. Integer
35. Line Graph
36. Numeral
37. Octagon
38. Operation
39. Ordinal
40. Ounce
41. Parallel
42. Plane
43. Percent
44. Polygon
45. Problem
46. Product
47. Quadrilateral
48. Quadruple
49. Quintuple
50. Region
51. Relationship
52. Remainder
53. Represent
54. Result
55. Reverse
56. Rhombus
57. Right Angle
58. Rounding
59. Simple
60. Surface
61. Table
62. Temperature
63. Thermometer
64. Ton
65. Undo
66. Union
67. Unknown
68. Unnamed
69. Vertical
70. Volume
71. Volume
72. Whole number
73. Skip counting
74. Solve
75. Sequence

3rd Grade Science (Bricks) Academic Vocabulary List

1. Airborne
2. Boil
3. Brain
4. Comet
5. Complex
6. Current
7. Cycle
8. Dissolve
9. Earthquake
10. Eclipse
11. Evidence
12. Fertilizer
13. Flow
14. Food Chain
15. Fossil
16. Friction
17. Gravity
18. Heart
19. Hemisphere
20. Horizon
21. Incisor
22. Intestines
23. Joint
24. Lava
25. Liver
26. Lungs
27. Microscope
28. Model
29. Molar
30. Motion
31. Neptune
32. Nutrients
33. Orbit
34. Organs
35. Oxygen
36. Planets
37. Plastic
38. Pollution
39. Protein
40. Pure
41. Reflexes
42. Simple
43. Solar System
44. Solution
45. Steam
46. Stem
47. Survive
48. System
49. Telescope
50. Volcano

3rd Grade Language Arts (Bricks) Academic Vocabulary List

1. Article
2. Base Word
3. Bias
4. Caption
5. Colon
6. Compare
7. Compound Noun
8. Context
9. Context Clue
10. Contraction
11. Contrast
12. Debate
13. Description
14. Dialogue
15. Dipthong
16. Essay
17. Fable
18. Format
19. Genre
20. Gist
21. Hieroglyphics
22. Homonym
23. Interrogative
24. Interviews
25. Introduction
26. Literature circle
27. Morpheme
28. Narrator
29. Parts of Speech
30. Pitch
31. Possessive
32. Possessive nouns
33. Predicate
34. Prediction
35. Preface
36. Prefixes
37. Preposition
38. Prior Knowledge
39. Relevant
40. Rhythm
41. Root word
42. Run-on sentence
43. Semi-colon
44. Subject
45. Suffixes
46. Summarize
47. Supporting details
48. Tall tale
49. Verb
50. Word Study

Chapter Ten:

Fourth Grade Academic Language & Academic Vocabulary

"He who opens a school door,
Closes a prison"

Victor Hugo

While students by fourth grade may have "learned to read" or decode effectively, they struggle to "read to learn" or comprehend effectively. Pearson (2007) points out that many fourth graders hit what he calls the fourth grade "reading slump." This is the point where a lack of academic language and vocabulary catches up with students. Because they do not have a large enough vocabulary to meet the demands of fourth grade level books, they find that reading becomes difficult and less enjoyable. This lack of comprehension can quickly lead to an aversion to reading. At the same time other students who have a sizable vocabulary and mastery of academic language seem to just take off in school. It seems the gap in achievement starts to get wider and the students who fall into the fourth grade "reading slump" start to show signs of being at least one or two grade levels behind. While it is exciting to see many students take off with their comprehension and appreciation for school, there are many other students who feel deflated and even defeated by the demands of reading and school. These students need a variety of targeted literacy interventions and continued language interventions in order to overcome the fourth grade "reading slump."

4th Grade (Mortar) Johnson Academic Language List

1. Additionally
2. Adjust
3. Afterwards
4. Anticipate
5. Apply
6. Approve
7. Assist
8. Attitude
9. Authority
10. Character
11. College
12. Concept
13. Conserve
14. Culture
15. Curriculum
16. Defend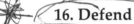
17. Devote
18. Dialogue
19. Document
20. Eliminate
21. Emphasize
22. Equality
23. Evaluate
24. Evidence
25. Examine
26. Exchange
27. Exercise
28. Exhibit
29. Express
30. Feedback
31. Fine-tune
32. For example
33. Frame
34. Frequently
35. Gauge
36. Host
37. Importantly
38. Inform
39. Inspire
40. Lecture
41. License
42. Lighten
43. Log
44. Mean
45. Mention
46. Motivate
47. Nurture
48. Operate
49. Portfolio
50. Prevent
51. Principles
52. Produce
53. Range
54. Rather
55. Reality
56. Reason
57. Reduce
58. Relate
59. Release
60. Replace
61. Represent
62. Research
63. Result
64. Retain
65. Schedule
66. Signify
67. Similarly
68. Sometimes
69. Stimulate
70. Strengthen
71. Structure
72. Supervise
73. Technology
74. Translate
75. Update

4th Grade Social Science (Bricks) Academic Vocabulary List

1. Accent
2. Adobe
3. Agriculture
4. Altitude
5. Ancestor
6. Ancient
7. Atmosphere
8. Attitude
9. Barter
10. Basic Needs
11. Cacao
12. Caste System
13. Cavalry
14. Central
15. City Ordinance
16. Civilian
17. Climate
18. Colony
19. Congress
20. Conservation
21. Constitution
22. Council
23. Culture
24. Current
25. Declaration
26. Demand
27. Democracy
28. Democrat
29. Depression
30. Dike
31. Economy
32. Efficient
33. Empire
34. Energy
35. Features
36. Fiber
37. Foreigner
38. Glacier
39. Goods
40. Habit
41. Independence
42. Industry
43. Information
44. Laborer
45. Lawmakers
46. Loom
47. Map Legend
48. Material
49. Mechanical
50. Mesa
51. Mineral
52. Missions
53. Modern
54. Monsoon
55. Partnership
56. Power Generator
57. Precipitation
58. Progressive
59. Raw Goods
60. Representative
61. Republican
62. Reservoir
63. Residential
64. Revolution
65. Shelter
66. Skills
67. Specialization
68. Supply
69. Symbols
70. Taxation
71. Textiles
72. Trade Winds
73. Vegetation
74. Era
75. Riot

4th Grade Mathematics (Bricks) Academic Vocabulary List

1. Acre
2. Adjacent
3. Align
4. Alternate
5. Arc
6. Arithmetic
7. Average
8. Bar
9. Bar Graph
10. Billion
11. Bracket
12. Calculate (lation)
13. Carat
14. Century
15. Cheap (est)
16. Circumference
17. Closed
18. Closure Property
19. Code
20. Collection
21. Combine
22. Common Factor
23. Commutative Operation
24. Compass
25. Complete
26. Complex
27. Conclusion
28. Congruent
29. Consecutive
30. Construct
31. Copy
32. Correct
33. Correspond
34. Cross
35. Decade
36. Decimal
37. Decimal place
38. Decrease

39. Degree
40. Denominator
41. Depth
42. Diagram
43. Distributive property
44. Divisibility
45. Expand
46. Form
47. Fraction
48. Function
49. Geometry
50. Gram
51. Grid
52. Half-circle
53. Identity property
54. Incorrect
55. Increase
56. Infinite
57. Liter
58. Meter
59. Millennium
60. Multiplier
61. Natural number
62. Numerator
63. Open
64. Ordered pairs
65. Parentheses
66. Percentage
67. Plane
68. Prime number
69. Product
70. Quantity
71. Radius
72. Ray
73. Reduce
74. Reflexive property
75. Transitive property

4th Grade Science (Bricks) Academic Vocabulary List

1. Abdomen
2. Accurate
3. Anatomy
4. Aorta
5. Artery
6. Atmosphere
7. Bedrock
8. Bicep
9. Bone marrow
10. Brain stem
11. Calcium
12. Carbon
13. Cell
14. Chemicals
15. Chlorine
16. Combination
17. Constellation
18. Core
19. Crust
20. Cylinder
21. Decay
22. Detector
23. Digestion
24. Embryo
25. Erosion
26. Evaporate
27. Formula
28. Geyser
29. Gills
30. Humidity
31. Insect
32. Launch
33. Light Year
34. Mantle
35. Mass
36. Matter
37. Membrane
38. Metric system
39. Model
40. Nervous system
41. Nucleus
42. Overpopulation
43. Phase
44. Pitch
45. Reproduce
46. Species
47. Stabilize
48. Structure
49. Volume
50. White blood cell

4ᵗʰ Grade Language Arts (Bricks) Academic Vocabulary List

1. Action verb
2. Affixes
3. Almanac
4. Aloof
5. Articulation
6. Author's purpose
7. Citation
8. Clause
9. Collage
10. Communication
11. Complement
12. Complex Sentence
13. Compound Sentence
14. Compound-Complex
15. Conjunctions
16. Conventions
17. Conversation
18. Declarative Sentence
19. Digraph
20. Direct object
21. Double-negative
22. Drawing conclusions
23. Exclamatory Sentence
24. Grammar
25. Helping verb
26. Imperative Sentence
27. Index
28. Indirect object
29. Inference
30. Interjections
31. Interrogative Sentence
32. Linking verb
33. Multi-syllabic
34. Novel
35. Object of sentence
36. Onset
37. Oral
38. Outline
39. Paraphrasing
40. Proofread
41. Quotations
42. Rate
43. Rime
44. Stanza
45. Subject/verb agreement
46. Thesaurus
47. Time order
48. Tone
49. Topic sentence
50. Verb tense

Chapter Eleven:
Fifth Grade Academic Language
& Academic Vocabulary

*"I like a teacher who gives you
something to take home to think
about besides homework."*

Lily Tomlin

By fifth grade textbooks start to become a larger part of schooling. By this age students are typically given a social studies textbook, a math textbook, a science textbook, and a language arts textbook. The amount of information a student is supposed to process and learn steadily increases. A growing amount of information is readily available in bookstores and libraries. It would seem that at our current time in history when there are mountains of information available at the touch of a keystroke on the internet that academic literacy would increase. Data, facts, and figures seem to surround us, yet academic literacy seems to escape so many learners as they drop out of school and shun the process that may serve as the means for creating an economically viable future. It almost seems as data and information increases, that for some student's their academic language and academic literacy decreases. While their language and literacy do not decrease, for many fifth graders the gap between their language and literacy skills lags even further behind the demands of textbooks and grade level reading expectations. Many fifth grade students need support in their academic language skills in order to keep up with the increasing grade level standards.

Academic Language & Academic Vocabulary

5th Grade (Mortar) Johnson Academic Language List

1. Approach	39. Manage
2. Automatically	40. Maximize
3. Besides	41. Meanwhile
4. Bias	42. Medical
5. Challenge	43. Narrate
6. Collaborate	44. Navigate
7. Collate	45. On the other hand
8. Commit	46. Opinion
9. Compile	47. Perfect
10. Conclude	48. Preserve
11. Conduct	49. Primarily
12. Conscious	50. Probability
13. Consequence	51. Reason
14. Content	52. Refine
15. Enable	53. Remodel
16. Engage	54. Repair
17. Environment	55. Reserve
18. Equip	56. Respond
19. Establish	57. Restrict
20. Even though	58. Retain
21. Ever Since	59. Sample
22. Expand	60. Screen
23. Expert	61. Series
24. Explain	62. Simplify
25. Extend	63. Still
26. Feature	64. Straighten
27. Fee	65. Submit
28. Forecast	66. Surely
29. Furthermore	67. Symbolic
30. In order that	68. Synthesize
31. Influence	69. System
32. Inspect	70. Technical
33. Install	71. Thus
34. Insure	72. Transform
35. Involve	73. Uncover
36. Issue	74. Unify
37. Launch	75. Upgrade
38. Maintain	

5th Grade Social Science (Bricks) Academic Vocabulary List

1. Administration
2. Agreement
3. Alabama
4. Alaska
5. Arizona
6. Arkansas
7. California
8. Chronicle
9. Coastline
10. Colorado
11. Connecticut
12. Continental Divide
13. Delaware
14. Erie Canal
15. Expansionism
16. Florida
17. Fortifications
18. Generation
19. Georgia
20. Hawaii
21. Heritage
22. Hierarchy
23. Idaho
24. Illinois
25. Indiana
26. Inhabitant
27. Invasion
28. Iowa
29. Kansas
30. Kentucky
31. Labor
32. Lewis & Clark Expedition
33. Louisiana
34. Maine
35. Manor
36. Martyr
37. Maryland
38. Massachusetts

39. Mayans
40. Michigan
41. Minnesota
42. Mississippi
43. Missouri
44. Montana
45. Nebraska
46. Nevada
47. New Hampshire
48. New Jersey
49. New Mexico
50. New York
51. North Carolina
52. North Dakota
53. Ohio
54. Oklahoma
55. Oregon
56. Pennsylvania
57. Press
58. Proposal
59. Province
60. Rhode Island
61. Security
62. Slavery
63. South Carolina
64. South Dakota
65. Strike
66. Tennessee
67. Texas
68. Utah
69. Vermont
70. Virginia
71. Washington
72. West Virginia
73. Wisconsin
74. Working class
75. Wyoming

5th Grade Mathematics (Bricks) Academic Vocabulary List

1. Actual
2. Acute angle
3. Additive
4. Array
5. Axis
6. Benchmark
7. Binary
8. Bisect
9. Break apart
10. Bushel
11. Capacity
12. Centigrade
13. Centigram
14. Centiliter
15. Compact numeral
16. Computation
17. Concentric
18. Constant
19. Convert
20. Coordinate axis
21. Crease
22. Currency
23. Data
24. Deca-
25. Deci-
26. Deka-
27. Deposit
28. Determine
29. Discount
30. Dot Graph
31. Duplicate
32. Egyptian numerals
33. Equiangular
34. Equilateral
35. Equivalent
36. Error
37. Event
38. Exact
39. Express (ion)
40. Face Value
41. Factor
42. Farther
43. Formula
44. Frequency
45. Full
46. Gain
47. Generalization
48. Gram
49. Greatest
50. Gross
51. Hemisphere
52. Heptagon
53. Hexahedron
54. Interest
55. Intersect
56. Kilo-
57. Loss
58. Mean
59. Median
60. Milli-
61. Mode
62. Obtuse angle
63. Partial
64. Place holder
65. Profit
66. Right triangle
67. Scale
68. Square root
69. Squared
70. Tally mark
71. Three-dimensional
72. Two-dimensional
73. Vertex (tices)
74. X-Axis
75. Y-Axis

5th Grade Science (Bricks) Academic Vocabulary List

1. Absorb
2. Acid
3. Astronomy
4. Atom
5. Audio
6. Celsius
7. Compound
8. Condensation
9. Coral Reef
10. Dew Point
11. Electric Charge
12. Filament
13. Geology
14. Germs
15. Glacier
16. Glucose
17. Habitat
18. Hibernate
19. Impulse
20. Indicator
21. Infection
22. Jupiter
23. Kidney
24. Mars
25. Mercury
26. Momentum
27. Nerve
28. Neutron
29. Optic Nerve
30. Photosynthesis
31. Pigment
32. Pluto
33. Predator
34. Pressure
35. Prey
36. Prism
37. Quarry
38. Radiant
39. Response
40. Saturn
41. Solar Energy
42. Sterilize
43. Stimulus
44. Substance
45. Tendon
46. Universe
47. Uranus
48. Valve
49. Vein
50. Venus

5th Grade Language Arts (Bricks) Academic Vocabulary List

1. Acronym
2. Citations
3. Cognates
4. Comparative
5. Decipher
6. Demonstrative Pronoun
7. Dependent clause
8. Epic
9. Falling action
10. Figurative language
11. Footnotes
12. Henchmen
13. Homograph
14. Hyperbole
15. Idiom
16. Implied
17. Indefinite Pronoun
18. Independent Clause
19. Interrogative Pronoun
20. Misnomer
21. Mnemonic Device
22. Modifier
23. Newspapers
24. Object of preposition
25. Onomatopoeia
26. Oral presentation
27. Palindrome
28. Personal Pronoun
29. Personification
30. Persuasive writing
31. Portfolio
32. Power
33. Prepositional phrase
34. Prompt
35. Quest
36. Reading log
37. Reference source
38. Relative Pronoun
39. Resolution
40. Retention
41. Rising action
42. Script
43. Sidekick
44. Subordinate Clause
45. Subtext
46. Text features
47. Theme
48. Thesis statement
49. True Love
50. Visual image

Chapter Twelve:

Sixth Grade Academic Language & Academic Vocabulary

"Education is learning what you didn't even know you didn't know."

Daniel Boorstin

Sixth grade students are making the transition from elementary school to middle school. The textbook becomes a bigger part of the academic equation, and those students who can negotiate the demands of textbooks typically do better in school. While some students maintain a high confidence in their ability to read and learn, others have a decreasing spiral of confidence. A situation called the "Matthew Effect" really starts to kick in. Those that can read well start to read more and more and become more confident as a learner, while those who struggle to read find themselves reading less and less and the lose confidence as a learner. In many ways, the academically rich (those with a rich vocabulary) become richer, while the academically poor (those who lack grade level academic language) become poorer. The behavior of these frustrated students who lack vocabulary confidence can often be difficult in class. These students can often begin to actively avoid reading, doing classwork, finishing homework, because they find reading to be a difficult chore. Without help and effective interventions these students may find that they push themselves further and further away from school.

6th Grade (Mortar) Johnson Academic Language List

1. Abstract
2. Accumulate
3. Assume
4. Boost
5. Career
6. Certainly
7. Cite
8. Civil
9. Clause
10. Component
11. Conceptualize
12. Concrete
13. Console
14. Contact
15. Contrastingly
16. Currently
17. Dedicate
18. Defer
19. Diagnose
20. Differentiate
21. Discharge
22. Effective
23. Efficient
24. Enlarge
25. Enlist
26. Even when
27. Expand
28. Extract
29. File
30. Filter
31. Finalize
32. Habit
33. Initially
34. Institute
35. Integrate
36. Likelihood
37. Localize
38. Logic
39. Mediate
40. Mentor
41. Merge
42. Metaphor
43. Modify
44. Moral
45. Notify
46. Obtain
47. Occupation
48. Perceive
49. Perhaps
50. Preside
51. Reaction
52. Reference
53. Regulate
54. Relevance
55. Reorganize
56. Response
57. Restore
58. Scheme
59. Scope
60. Sequentially
61. Significantly
62. Simultaneously
63. Spearhead
64. Specialize
65. Survey
66. Tense
67. Therefore
68. Transfer
69. Transmit
70. Undertake
71. Unveil
72. Value
73. Version
74. Viewpoint
75. Witness

6th Grade Social Science (Bricks) Academic Vocabulary List

1. Adapt
2. Affluence
3. Agent
4. Alamo
5. Allegiance
6. Amendment
7. Ancient
8. Appeal
9. Aqueduct
10. Archaeology
11. Architecture
12. Authority
13. Automation
14. Aviation
15. Behavior
16. Bias
17. Boycott
18. Cash Crop
19. Chief Executive Officer
20. Civilization
21. Colonist
22. Congo
23. Consumer
24. Credit
25. Department
26. Diet
27. Federal
28. Flint
29. Founding fathers
30. Fur trade
31. Industry
32. Institution
33. Interchangeable
34. Investment
35. Israel
36. Journalist
37. Kuwait
38. Latitude
39. Liberation
40. Longitude
41. Madagascar
42. Majority
43. Manufacturing
44. Merchant
45. Middle class
46. Middle East
47. Minority
48. Missionary
49. Mozambique
50. Native
51. Nigeria
52. Oral History
53. Palestinian
54. Pilgrim
55. Plantation
56. Politics
57. Poverty
58. Prime Meridian
59. Puritan
60. Quaker
61. Radical
62. Reservation
63. Resources
64. Ruins
65. Russia
66. Samoa
67. Saudi Arabia
68. Savannah
69. Society
70. South Africa
71. System
72. Treaty
73. Ukraine
74. Unions
75. Yemen

6th Grade Mathematics (Bricks) Academic Vocabulary List

1. Algorithm
2. Altitude
3. Annex
4. Chord
5. Circumscribed
6. Collinear
7. Composite
8. Cross-Product
9. Cross-Section
10. Cryptogram
11. Cubed
12. Cubic Measurement
13. Cubit
14. Denote
15. Density
16. Distribution
17. Dodecahedron
18. Element
19. Estimation
20. Extend
21. Fathom
22. Finite Set
23. First Power
24. Fixed
25. Flat
26. Fluid
27. Frame
28. Function
29. Given
30. Halved
31. Hypotenuse
32. If-then Rule
33. If-then-not Rule
34. Include
35. Indent
36. Input
37. Inscribed
38. Insert
39. Interest Rate
40. Interval
41. Inverse
42. Isosceles
43. Lattice Method
44. Layer
45. Least Common Denominator
46. Linear
47. Locate
48. Magic Square
49. Magic Sum
50. Maximum
51. Micron
52. Miles Per Hour
53. Minimum
54. Nonstandard
55. Original
56. Output
57. Precise
58. Prime Number
59. Primer Factor
60. Principal
61. Prism
62. Probability
63. Progression
64. Projection
65. Proportion
66. Protractor
67. Pyramid
68. Quartiles
69. Ratios
70. Reverse
71. Scale
72. Scalene triangle
73. Surface
74. Symmetry
75. Terminating

6th Grade Science (Bricks) Academic Vocabulary List

1. Algae
2. Aluminum
3. Amphibian
4. Ceramic
5. Chemistry
6. Cirrus
7. Conductor
8. Cortex
9. Cumulonimbus
10. Cumulus
11. Deciduous
12. Deficiency
13. Diaphragm
14. Dominant
15. Embalm
16. Emission
17. Fault Line
18. Fungus
19. Galaxy
20. Gall Bladder
21. Generator
22. Gland
23. Granite
24. Hypothesis
25. Igneous
26. Inertia
27. Limestone
28. Mutation
29. Nimbus
30. Organism
31. Pancreas
32. Particle
33. Permanent
34. Physics
35. Pigment
36. Pistil
37. Pollinate
38. Primitive
39. Propane
40. Ray
41. Resistance
42. Sedimentary Rock
43. Seep
44. State
45. Stress
46. Thermal
47. Transparent
48. Virus
49. Wavelength
50. X-ray

6th Grade Science (Bricks) Academic Vocabulary List

1. Analogy
2. Antecedent
3. Clarity
4. Clauses
5. Employ
6. Figurative
7. Foreign phrases
8. Future tense
9. Homophone
10. Hyperbole
11. Imagery
12. Inference
13. Intransitive verb
14. Irregular verbs
15. Irrelevant
16. Journal
17. Literal
18. Meter
19. Moral
20. Multiple meanings
21. Past tense
22. Pertinent
23. Poignant
24. Point of view
25. Position
26. Primary source
27. Propaganda
28. Relevancy
29. Rhyme
30. Rhythm
31. Secondary source
32. Sequential order
33. Sidebars
34. Stressed/unstressed
35. Superlatives
36. Syllabication
37. Syllables
38. Symbolism
39. Syntax
40. Terse
41. Text features
42. Thesis statement
43. Tome
44. Transitive verb
45. Trivial
46. Unorthodox
47. Vacillate
48. Verbal
49. Voice
50. Writing modes

Chapter Thirteen:

Seventh Grade Academic Language
& Academic Vocabulary

*"I am indebted to my father for living
but to my teacher for living well."*

Alexander the Great

Seventh grade can be a challenging time for any student. Expectations rise rapidly in areas of responsibility. Seventh graders typically have multiple teachers in different content areas. The personalization of elementary school is often gone and students are expected to do more homework and individual assignments to demonstrate their learning. Seventh grade students who have the academic language and the ability to learn more academic language typically do just fine in school. At the same time, students who lack academic language and vocabulary find that school becomes very difficult. For many the textbook is a burden and homework often seems overwhelming. If these students are provided literacy strategies (inferring, structured discussion, academic talk, etc.) and language strategies (academic language graphic organizers, word lists, fist-to-five, etc.), then they can begin to bridge the gap in their language and eventually in their achievement. On the other hand, Pearson (2007) emphasizes that any students will fall off of the seventh grade "reading cliff." Most students who fall of the seventh grade reading cliff struggle to comprehend and they have less and less confidence in their ability to succeed in school.

7th Grade (Mortar) Johnson Academic Language List

1. Adapt
2. Allocate
3. Although
4. Analogy
5. Appoint
6. As a result
7. Awareness
8. Coincidentally
9. Comment
10. Contend
11. Correspond
12. Counsel
13. Criteria
14. Cultivate
15. Customize
16. Disclose
17. Dispatch
18. Diversify
19. Element
20. Enforce
21. Engineer
22. Enhance
23. Enrich
24. Ensure
25. Eventually
26. Fabricate
27. For instance
28. Formulate
29. Fortify
30. Framework
31. Further
32. Furthermore
33. Illustrate
34. Impart
35. In spite of
36. Indeed
37. Initiate
38. Insight
39. Integrity
40. Intermediate
41. Intervene
42. Justify
43. Likewise
44. Mean
45. Median
46. Minimize
47. Minority
48. Mobilize
49. Mode
50. Moderate
51. Moreover
52. Mutual
53. Nonetheless
54. Officiate
55. Prioritize
56. Probe
57. Rehabilitate
58. Reinforce
59. Retain
60. Retrieve
61. Revise
62. Specify
63. Sphere
64. Stability
65. Strategy
66. Surpass
67. Sustain
68. Technique
69. Therefore
70. Transform
71. Upheld
72. Vary
73. Vitalize
74. Whereby
75. Withdraw

7th Grade Social Science (Bricks) Academic Vocabulary List

1. Algeria
2. Argentina
3. Basin
4. Bay
5. Belize
6. Blue-collar
7. Bolivia
8. Bosnia
9. Brazil
10. Bulgaria
11. Central America
12. Century
13. Chile
14. Class
15. Costa Rica
16. Cuneiform
17. Denmark
18. Dowry
19. Dynasty
20. Egypt
21. El Salvador
22. Equador
23. Estonia
24. Finland
25. Glacier
26. Greece
27. Guatemala
28. Gulf
29. Harbor
30. Honduras
31. Industrialization
32. Iran
33. Iraq
34. Irrigation
35. Jordan
36. Latvia
37. Lebanon
38. Liberty
39. Libya
40. Medieval
41. Middle Ages
42. Middle passage
43. Military
44. Morocco
45. Mountain Range
46. Mythology
47. Nazi
48. Nicaragua
49. Nomadic
50. Nominee
51. Norse Gods
52. Norway
53. Pact
54. Panama Canal
55. Peru
56. Plains
57. Political party
58. Qatar
59. Red Sea
60. Refugee
61. Renaissance
62. Republic
63. Revolutionary War
64. Saint
65. Scandinavia
66. South America
67. Steppe
68. Sudan
69. Suez Canal
70. Syria
71. Technology
72. Tunisia
73. Turkey
74. White-collar
75. Yemen

7th Grade Mathematics (Bricks) Academic Vocabulary List

1. Additive inverse
2. Algebraic expression
3. Asymmetrical
4. Cancel Out
5. Centroid
6. Commission
7. Concave
8. Convex
9. Derive
10. Disjoint
11. Ellipse
12. Expanded notation
13. Exterior
14. Extrapolation
15. Foci
16. Fortnight
17. Furlong
18. Graduated scale
19. Half-plane
20. Histogram
21. Icosahedron
22. Identity element
23. Inclusion
24. Inclusive
25. Infinity
26. Interior
27. Intersect
28. Inverse
29. Lateral
30. Leap year
31. Least common multiple
32. Light year
33. Line plot
34. Linear equation
35. Linear inequality
36. Lower limit
37. Markup
38. Minuend
39. Outcome
40. Parallelogram
41. Platonic solids
42. Pythagorean theorem
43. Quadrillion
44. Quintillion
45. Quotient
46. Radian
47. Range
48. Rate
49. Reciprocal
50. Reduction
51. Reference line
52. Regular
53. Result
54. Rotation
55. Scientific notation
56. Segment
57. Separate
58. Simplify
59. Solution
60. Space
61. Sphere
62. Subset
63. Substitute
64. System
65. Transversal
66. Trapezoid
67. Trillion
68. Two-Stage Problem
69. Undivided
70. Upper Limit
71. Variable
72. Volume
73. Weigh
74. Zero Power
75. Zillion

7th Grade Science (Bricks) Academic Vocabulary List

1. Adrenaline
2. Aerobic
3. Agronomy
4. Air Resistance
5. Alloy
6. Amino Acid
7. Botany
8. Cellulose
9. Chromosome
10. Circuit
11. Contraction
12. Decelerate
13. Diagnosis
14. Ecology
15. Electric Current
16. Element
17. Fission
18. Formaldehyde
19. Fusion
20. Genes
21. Gland
22. Hazardous
23. Heredity
24. Life Cycle
25. Liver
26. Magma
27. Melting Point
28. Methane
29. Microorganism
30. Molecule
31. Natural Gas
32. Organic
33. Ovary
34. Periodic Table
35. Potassium
36. Protozoan
37. Puberty
38. Receptor
39. Regenerate
40. Respiration
41. Saturation
42. Sediment
43. Semiconductor
44. Sperm Cell
45. Stethoscope
46. Tremor
47. Turbine
48. Variation
49. Voltage
50. Water shed

7th Grade Language Arts (Bricks) Academic Vocabulary List

1. Adverbial Phrase
2. Adjective Phrase
3. Accent
4. Assonance
5. Causation
6. Classics
7. Climax
8. Connotation
9. Consonance
10. Denotation
11. Double-negative
12. Epilogue
13. Etymology
14. First Person
15. Flashback
16. Foreign phrases
17. Foreshadowing
18. Inferences
19. Interaction with texts
20. Internal rhyme
21. Irony
22. Juncture
23. Limited Omniscient
24. Metaphor
25. Mood
26. Narration
27. Nuance
28. Objective
29. Omniscient
30. Onomatopoeia
31. Paraphrase
32. Perspective
33. Pitch
34. Proofread
35. Repetition
36. Second Person
37. Semantic change
38. Short Story
39. Simile
40. Stress
41. Superlative
42. Third Person
43. Tone
44. Transcribe
45. Verse
46. Viewpoint
47. Parody
48. Sensory detail
49. Shades of meaning
50. Transitional words

Chapter Fourteen:

Eighth Grade Academic Language & Academic Vocabulary

*"There is more treasure in books than in
all the pirate's loot on Treasure Island."*

Walt Disney

Eighth grade is an important turning point for students. It is typically their last year of middle school and by the end of the year they will be transitioning to high school. This is the point where many students start to think about dropping out. We are seeing more and more eighth graders dropping out of school, yet most students wait to see how things go in high school before they make any fateful decisions. By this point it can be easier to see which students who are at significant risk of dropping out and discontinuing their education. Students who lack academic language and literacy skills avoid reading textbooks, their attitude and behavior towards school is often poor as a result, and they often do not finish homework. As a result, these students are typically at least two grade levels behind. Many are only reading at a fourth grade level, yet they will soon be expected to read high school textbooks. These students feel the crunch and weight of the language and the achievement gap, and they often look for opportunities outside school to find achievement. For many students, unless they see a significant increase in their academic language and literacy skills, they will take their lack of confidence to the next level knowing they are ill-equipped to deal with the demands of high school.

8th Grade (Mortar) Johnson Academic Language List

1. Affect
2. Amend
3. Analogy
4. Annually
5. Anticipate
6. Appraise
7. Aspect
8. Assure
9. Attain
10. Benefit
11. Broaden
12. Characteristic
13. Circumstance
14. Commodity
15. Confer
16. Conform
17. Consult
18. Context
19. Controversy
20. Conversely
21. Criteria
22. Devote
23. Dimension
24. Dissect
25. Domain
26. Doubtless
27. Element
28. Enlighten
29. Enumerate
30. Ethics
31. Facilitate
32. Familiarize
33. Federal
34. Flexibility
35. Foster
36. Fundamental
37. Hypothesis
38. Identical
39. Import
40. Improvise
41. Incorporate
42. Individualize
43. Initially
44. Innovate
45. Issue
46. Just as
47. Literacy
48. Meantime
49. Modify
50. Nevertheless
51. Notion
52. Offset
53. Opposing
54. Overall
55. Overhaul
56. Perspective
57. Phenomenon
58. Philosophy
59. Policy
60. Promote
61. Regardless
62. Render
63. Resolve
64. Retain
65. Scenario
66. Secure
67. Segment
68. Simulate
69. Statistic
70. Status
71. Subsequently
72. Thesis
73. Though
74. Variable
75. Visualize

8th Grade Social Science (Bricks) Academic Vocabulary List

1. Abolitionist
2. Advertise
3. Agrarian
4. Alliance
5. Altruism
6. Amazon River
7. Anthropology
8. Assassination
9. Belgium
10. Bilingual
11. Black Sea
12. Boycott
13. Budget
14. Bureau
15. Cabinet
16. Commerce
17. Conservative
18. Consumption
19. Corruption
20. Cotton Gin
21. Covenant
22. Cuba
23. Czar
24. Delegation
25. Desegregation
26. Doctrine
27. Ellis Island
28. Emancipation proclamation
29. Embargo
30. England
31. Epidemic
32. Epoch
33. Exodus
34. France
35. Freeman's bureau
36. Germany
37. Great Britain
38. Gulf of Mexico
39. Himalayas
40. Hudson Bay
41. Ice cap
42. Ireland
43. Italy
44. Liberal
45. Luxembourg
46. Netherlands
47. Pardon
48. Philanthropy
49. Phoenicians
50. Populist
51. Portugal
52. Psychology
53. Pyrenees
54. Reconstruction
55. Regime
56. Reservation
57. Sacred
58. Scotland
59. Sociology
60. Spain
61. St. Lawrence River
62. Strategy
63. Subculture
64. Superpower
65. Switzerland
66. Tactics
67. Terrorism
68. Theology
69. Tolerance
70. Topographical
71. Trail of Tears
72. Tundra
73. Unification
74. Utopia
75. Wales

8th Grade Algebra (Bricks) Academic Vocabulary List

1. Absolute value
2. Additive inverse
3. Argand plane
4. Closed interval
5. Coefficient
6. Combinatorics
7. Compatible matrices
8. Complex conjugate
9. Compound interest
10. Compression
11. Conditional equation
12. Conic sections
13. Constant
14. Contrapositive
15. Convergent series
16. Cube root
17. Cubic polynomial
18. Dilation
19. Direct variation
20. Directly proportional
21. Discriminant of a quadratic
22. Distinct
23. Domain of definition
24. Doubling time
25. Echelon form of a matrix
26. Expand
27. Exponent
28. Extraneous solution
29. Extreme values
30. Factorial
31. Floor function
32. Focal radius
33. Foci of a hyperbola
34. FOIL method
35. Fractional expression
36. Gaussian elimination
37. Greatest common factor
38. Greatest integer function
39. Half-life
40. Half-open interval
41. Harmonic series
42. Horizontal sift
43. Horizontal translation
44. Identity matrix
45. Imaginary part
46. Independence variable
47. Interval notation
48. Inversely proportional
49. Joint variation
50. Leading coefficient
51. Like terms
52. Locus
53. Logarithm
54. Magnitude
55. Matrix
56. Monomial
57. Non-real numbers
58. Permutation
59. Projectile motion
60. Quadratic equation
61. Quartic polynomial
62. Radical
63. Relatively prime
64. Restricted function
65. Root rules
66. Scientific notation
67. Simultaneous equations
68. Spurious solution
69. Surd
70. Tau
71. Transformations
72. Trinomial
73. Triple root
74. Undefined slope
75. Vertical ellipse

8th Grade Science (Bricks) Academic Vocabulary List

1. Accelerate
2. Air Pressure
3. Antibiotic
4. Aorta
5. Artery
6. Beta
7. Biopsy
8. Bone-marrow
9. Calories
10. Capillaries
11. Catalyst
12. Chromium
13. Clone
14. Cornea
15. Corrosive
16. Cross-pollinate
17. Decompose
18. Electrode
19. Enzyme
20. Epidemic
21. Fabricate
22. Fulcrum
23. Galvanometer
24. Hemoglobin
25. Inflammation
26. Inherit
27. Insulator
28. Kinetic Energy
29. Light Spectrum
30. Lobe
31. Magnetic Field
32. Malaria
33. Mitochondria
34. Nitrate
35. Nodules
36. Ohm
37. Parasite
38. Penicillin
39. Permafrost
40. Quartz
41. Radioactive
42. Retina
43. Satellite
44. Secretion
45. Seismic
46. Stamen
47. Static Electricity
48. Stethoscope
49. Ventricle
50. Water Table

8th Grade Language Arts (Bricks) Academic Vocabulary List

1. Allusion
2. Antecedent
3. Aside
4. Ballad
5. Blank Verse
6. Climax
7. Clincher sentence
8. Coherent
9. Composition
10. Conflict
11. Couplet
12. Cross-reference
13. Deductive reasoning
14. Derivation
15. Dramatization
16. Elaboration
17. Emphasize
18. Endnotes
19. Enunciation
20. Exposition
21. Facilitator
22. Foot
23. Free Verse
24. Gerund
25. Haiku
26. Iamb
27. Iambic Pentameter
28. Inductive reasoning
29. Inferring
30. Infinitives
31. Inflection
32. Irony
33. Jargon
34. Limerick
35. Logic
36. Lyric Poem
37. Narrative Poem
38. Ode
39. Person vs. Person
40. Person vs. Nature
41. Person vs. Self
42. Participles
43. Point of View
44. Reliability
45. Sidebars
46. Sonnet
47. Stanza
48. Subplot
49. Tension
50. Verbals

Chapter Fifteen:

Ninth Grade Academic Language & Academic Vocabulary

*"Teachers open the door, but
you must enter by yourself."*

Chinese Proverb

Ninth grade is exciting for students as they enter high school and find more opportunities and responsibilities surround them. Students know that grades will now definitely count towards college entrance. Classes must be passed in order to make academic progress. Many students make this transition effectively and are on track for college if they so choose. At the same time there are many students who lack confidence as a learner, who find that they are failing all of their core classes. While they may be passing PE and Art with a "C", they have straight "F's" in algebra, language arts, earth science, and world geography. It seems like it is just a matter of time before a large majority of these students drop-out and become part of the 29% of students in America who fail to graduate on time. Of course for African-Americans and Latinos the percentage of drop-outs is over 40%. It is difficult to build back the confidence of these students, yet if they are to have any hope they will definitely need the academic language and vocabulary to help them succeed in school. Students can be assigned to academic support classes where they learn the academic words and intervention strategies to help negotiate the demands of independent learning that is associated with high school.

9th Grade (Mortar) Johnson Academic Language List

1. Abstract
2. Accommodate
3. Accordingly
4. Adequate
5. Align
6. Anticipate
7. Attain
8. Capacity
9. Chemical
10. Classical
11. Compatible
12. Comprise
13. Condense
14. Confirm
15. Contrarily
16. Conversely
17. Convert
18. Despite
19. Domestic
20. Dynamic
21. Eliminate
22. Erode
23. Estate
24. Explicit
25. Formulate
26. Function
27. Generalize
28. Guarantee
29. Harmonize
30. Hierarchy
31. However
32. Hypothesis
33. Implicit
34. Incorporate
35. Infinite
36. Infrastructure
37. Insight
38. Insight

39. Interpret
40. Investigate
41. Likewise
42. Mature
43. Meanwhile
44. Nonetheless
45. Orchestrate
46. Oversee
47. Parameter
48. Partnership
49. Portion
50. Practitioner
51. Precede
52. Propose
53. Protocol
54. Publicize
55. Randomly
56. Relevance
57. Reluctantly
58. Revitalize
59. Revolution
60. Satisfy
61. Somewhat
62. Standardize
63. Streamline
64. Stress
65. Successively
66. Symbolize
67. Synthesize
68. Temporarily
69. Tendency
70. Terminology
71. Theory
72. Thereby
73. Treatment
74. Ultimately
75. Vitalize

9th Grade Social Science (Bricks) Academic Vocabulary List

1. Afghanistan
2. Alps
3. Andes
4. Apartheid
5. Arabian
6. Aztecs
7. Bangladesh
8. Beliefs
9. Bhutan
10. Burma
11. Burma
12. Cambodia
13. Capital Goods
14. Carpathians
15. Caucasus
16. China
17. Chivalry
18. Conformity
19. Demographics
20. Denomination
21. Détente
22. Diversity
23. Divided
24. Emigrant
25. Fiji
26. Free Enterprise
27. Great Plains
28. Hinterlands
29. Hostility
30. India
31. Indonesia
32. Infrastructure
33. Innovation
34. Insurrection
35. Interdependence
36. Japan
37. Jihad
38. Kazakhstan
39. Kyrgystan
40. Laos
41. Malaysia
42. Mediterranean
43. Micronesia
44. Moderate
45. Mongolia
46. Mulatto
47. Nepal
48. Neutrality
49. New Zealand
50. Niger River
51. Nile River
52. North Korea
53. Pakistan
54. Phillipines
55. Scapegoat
56. Singapore
57. Social Norms
58. South Korea
59. Soviet
60. Sri Lanka
61. Succession
62. Tahiti
63. Taiwan
64. Tajikistan
65. Thailand
66. Tonga
67. Topography
68. Treaty
69. Tributary
70. Turkmenistan
71. Urbanization
72. Uzbekistan
73. Vernacular
74. Victorian
75. Vietnam

9th Grade Algebra (Bricks) Academic Vocabulary List

1. Absolute value
2. Additive inverse
3. Argand plane
4. Closed interval
5. Coefficient
6. Combinatorics
7. Compatible matrices
8. Complex conjugate
9. Compound interest
10. Compression
11. Conditional equation
12. Conic sections
13. Constant
14. Contrapositive
15. Convergent series
16. Cube root
17. Cubic polynomial
18. Dilation
19. Direct variation
20. Directly proportional
21. Discriminant of a quadratic
22. Distinct
23. Domain of definition
24. Doubling time
25. Echelon form of a matrix
26. Expand
27. Exponent
28. Extraneous solution
29. Extreme values
30. Factorial
31. Floor function
32. Focal radius
33. Foci of a hyperbola
34. FOIL method
35. Fractional expression
36. Gaussian elimination
37. Greatest common factor
38. Greatest integer function
39. Half-life
40. Half-open interval
41. Harmonic series
42. Horizontal sift
43. Horizontal translation
44. Identity matrix
45. Imaginary part
46. Independence variable
47. Interval notation
48. Inversely proportional
49. Joint variation
50. Leading 152oefficient
51. Like terms
52. Locus
53. Logarithm
54. Magnitude
55. Matrix
56. Monomial
57. Non-real numbers
58. Permutation
59. Projectile motion
60. Quadratic equation
61. Quartic polynomial
62. Radical
63. Relatively prime
64. Restricted function
65. Root rules
66. Scientific notation
67. Simultaneous equations
68. Spurious solution
69. Surd
70. Tau
71. Transformations
72. Trinomial
73. Triple root
74. Undefined slope
75. Vertical ellipse

9th Grade Science (Bricks) Academic Vocabulary List

1. Antibodies
2. Atomic Weight
3. Benign
4. Calculus
5. Carbohydrate
6. Carbon Dioxide
7. Cardiovascular
8. Carnivore
9. Classify
10. Dissection
11. Diverge
12. Ecosystem
13. Electromagnetic
14. Electron
15. Epilepsy
16. Esophagus
17. Evolve
18. Excretion
19. Fahrenheit
20. Herbivore
21. Hygiene
22. Inoculation
23. Lens
24. Lever
25. Lymphatic
26. Magneto
27. Metamorphic Rock
28. Molting
29. Neurosurgeon
30. Nitrogen
31. Omnivore
32. Pendulum
33. PH levels
34. Pituitary
35. Plasma
36. Pox
37. Pulmonary
38. Pupa
39. Radiation
40. Saliva
41. Seizure
42. Spore
43. Synthetic
44. Transplant
45. Tumor
46. Ultraviolet
47. Vacuum
48. Variable
49. Velocity
50. Vertebrate

9th Grade Language Arts (Bricks) Academic Vocabulary List

1. Allegory
2. Alliteration
3. Allusion
4. Appeal to Fear
5. Assonance
6. Audience
7. Antagonist
8. Anthology
9. Argumentation
10. Coherence
11. Consonance
12. Diction
13. Discourse
14. Drama
15. Elements of plot
16. Elements of poetry
17. Etymology
18. Explicit
19. Expository
20. False Analogy
21. False Dilemma
22. Figure of Speech
23. Foreign words
24. Foreshadowing
25. Gerund Phrase
26. Hyperbole
27. Imagery
28. Implicit
29. Improvisation
30. Infinitive Phrase
31. Logical fallacies
32. Monologue
33. Onomatopoeia
34. Oratory
35. Participial Phrase
36. Personal Attachment
37. Persuasive devices
38. Prose
39. Protagonist Questioning
40. Pun
41. Research
42. Revision
43. Rubric
44. Sarcasm
45. Soliloquy
46. Symbolism
47. Tertiary Source
48. Themes, recurring
49. Thesis
50. Understatement

Chapter Sixteen:

Tenth Grade Academic Language & Academic Vocabulary

"The dream begins with a teacher who believes in you, who tugs and pushes and leads you to the next plateau, sometimes poking you with a sharp stick called "truth".

Dan Rather

Many tenth graders who struggled through their freshman year take a wait and see approach to their sophomore year. If they can at least get a few "D's" and pass some classes they will stick in school, but if more failing grades come then they start to look for the door. Some of these students will try alternative high schools, but many will just follow many of the failing freshman and drop out to find opportunities on the street or in minimum-wage paying jobs. At the same time, tenth graders with large academic vocabularies are grappling with Advanced Placement (AP) World History and AP Biology classes. The gap between the academic haves and academic have nots seems to continue to widen. Many students who have struggled with the fourth grade "reading slump" and have fallen off the seventh grade "reading cliff" find themselves in the drop-out chasm that swallows up so many high school students. For those students still struggling to stay in school and make academic progress, bolstering their academic language and vocabulary will make the biggest difference.

10th Grade (Mortar) Johnson Academic Language List

1. Accelerate
2. Accordingly
3. Accumulate
4. Activate
5. Advise
6. Advocate
7. Affirm
8. Allocate
9. Appreciate
10. Arbitrate
11. Ascertain
12. Audit
13. Auditory
14. Augment
15. Avert
16. Bolster
17. Calibrate
18. Catalogue
19. Cater
20. Centralize
21. Cheer
22. Consolidate
23. Consolidate
24. Crucial
25. Debate
26. Depict
27. Depreciate
28. Derive
29. Devote
30. Differentiate
31. Disseminate
32. Dramatize
33. Elicit
34. Enrich
35. Envision
36. Excite
37. Exert
38. Extend
39. Extrapolate
40. Figurative
41. Foregoing
42. Hence
43. Ideology
44. Implement
45. Interface
46. Interpersonal
47. Literal
48. Litigate
49. Median
50. Meta-cognition
51. Mislead
52. Mode
53. Nevertheless
54. Nuance
55. Oppose
56. Orbit
57. Paraphrase
58. Perspective
59. Recap
60. Recommend
61. Retract
62. Revamp
63. Rubric
64. Scheme
65. Scrutinize
66. Simulation
67. Strategize
68. Systematize
69. Tabulate
70. Transcribe
71. Transpose
72. Troubleshoot
73. Trust
74. Verbal
75. Widespread

10th Grade Social Science (Bricks) Academic Vocabulary List

1. Abdicate
2. Age of Reason
3. Alliance
4. Amnesty
5. Anarchy
6. Annexation
7. Anti-Semitism
8. Aristocracy
9. Armistice
10. Assimilation
11. Autocracy
12. Black Plague
13. Buddhism
14. Byzantine Empire
15. Caste System
16. Catholicism
17. Code of Hammurabi
18. Confucianism
19. Coup
20. Crusades
21. Cultural Exchange
22. Dictatorship
23. Diplomacy
24. Discovery
25. English Bill of Rights
26. Enlightenment
27. Feudalism
28. French Revolution
29. Genocide
30. Greek Gods
31. Guerrilla Warfare
32. Hinterlands
33. Homogeneous
34. Humanism
35. Hunter Gatherers
36. Ice Age
37. Imperialism
38. Indentured Servant
39. Indigenous
40. Indus Valley
41. Industrialization
42. Islam
43. Judeo-Christian Ethic
44. Knight
45. Magna Charta
46. Marxism
47. Massacre
48. Mesopotamia
49. Militarism
50. Mobilize
51. Monarchy
52. Monastic
53. Monotheism
54. Nationalism
55. Neutrality
56. Polytheism
57. Protestantism
58. Reformation
59. Reparations
60. Roman Empire
61. Roman Gods
62. Romanticism
63. Samurai
64. Sanction
65. Serf
66. Social Darwinism
67. Sovereignty
68. Spice Trade
69. Stereotype
70. Taoism
71. Trench Warfare
72. Tyranny
73. Ultimatum
74. World War I
75. World War II

10th Grade Geography (Bricks) Academic Vocabulary List

1. Accuracy
2. Acute angle
3. Adjacent angle
4. Amplitude
5. Annulus
6. Apex
7. Apothem
8. Asymptote
9. Attitude
10. Bearing
11. Beta
12. Centroid
13. Circumcenter
14. Circumcircle
15. Circumscribed
16. Coincident
17. Complementary angles
18. Composite
19. Compression
20. Concentric
21. Concurrent
22. Contrapositive
23. Coplanar
24. Cos
25. Cosine
26. Cotangent
27. Coterminal
28. Cuboid
29. Decagon
30. Diametrically opposed
31. Dihedral angle
32. Dilation
33. Direct proportion
34. Distinct
35. Dodecagon
36. Euclidean
37. Fractal
38. Frustum
39. Glide reflection
40. Golden mean
41. Golden ratio
42. Heptagon
43. Hero's formula
44. Inscribed circle
45. Invariant
46. Inverse secant
47. Isometry
48. Kite
49. Lateral area
50. Magnitude
51. Major arc
52. Mensuration
53. Minor arc
54. Negative reciprocal
55. Noncollinear
56. Oblique
57. Ordered triple
58. Orthocenter
59. Parallel
60. Plus/minus identities
61. Radicand
62. Regular
63. Scale Factor
64. Secant
65. Simple harmonic motion
66. Sin
67. Sine
68. Sum/difference identities
69. Tan
70. Tangent
71. Theorem
72. Theta
73. Torus
74. Truncated cone of pyramid
75. Unit circle

10th Grade Science (Bricks) Academic Vocabulary List

1. Amoeba
2. Anemia
3. Anesthesia
4. Anomaly
5. Anterior
6. Antidote
7. Autonomic
8. Bacterium
9. Biodiversity
10. Cadaver
11. Composition
12. Concentration
13. Conservation
14. Density
15. Displacement
16. DNA
17. Entropy
18. Flagellum
19. Gamma rays
20. Genotype
21. Germination
22. Heterogeneous
23. Homeostasis
24. Homogeneous
25. Hormones
26. Infrared
27. Insulin
28. Invertebrate
29. Ligament
30. Meiosis
31. Mitosis
32. Osmosis
33. Pathogen
34. Pathology
35. Phenotype
36. Physiology
37. Pollen
38. Polymers
39. Precious Stones
40. Progesterone
41. Pulse Rate
42. Quantum theory
43. Radium
44. Range
45. Red blood cell
46. Somatic
47. Sulfur
48. Symbiotic
49. Torque
50. Vibration

10th Grade Science (Bricks) Academic Vocabulary List

1. Ambiguity
2. Antagonist
3. Archetype
4. Background Setting
5. Cliffhanger
6. Coalesce
7. Concise
8. Connotation
9. Contradiction
10. Denotation
11. Dilemma
12. Elements of argument
13. Elements of design
14. Elements of plot
15. Elements of prose
16. Epithet
17. Ethos
18. External Conflict
19. Fallacies
20. Flashback
21. Foil
22. Hyperbole
23. Implied Thesis
24. Incongruity
25. Integral Setting
26. Internal Conflict
27. Interpersonal Conflict
28. Juxtaposition
29. Logical fallacy
30. Logos
31. Modes of discourse
32. Open Ending
33. Parallelism
34. Pathos
35. Personal
36. Persuasive devices
37. Peruse
38. Protagonist
39. Ramble
40. Reasoning
41. Research
42. Rhetorical devices
43. Satire
44. Shift
45. Style
46. Subtle
47. Suspense
48. Time Lapse
49. Verbose
50. Vignette

Chapter Seventeen:
Eleventh Grade Academic Language
& Academic Vocabulary

"Personally I am always ready to learn,
Although I do not always
Like being taught."

Winston Churchill

The NAEP scores show that our eleventh grade students are seeing flat results over the past several years, while at the same time the high school drop-out rates are increasing. Without academic language and literacy the ability to organize, synthesize, and use this information becomes extremely difficult. Academic literacy requires active and engaged learners. In this glut of information there are television shows, video games, and You-Tube clips that provide plenty of passive entertainment, yet all of this video input is rather devoid of active learning. Students who have developed confidence as readers, because they have the academic language skills to learn independently will find they are on track to become "life-long learners." At the same time eleventh graders who lack confidence as readers and learners will fail to take advantage of the opportunities around them. They often sell themselves short and find that many doors are closed to them. Academic language provides the foundation for scaffolding life-long learning and literacy. Academic literacy provides a framework that is essential to developing specific content-area literacy.

11th Grade (Mortar) Johnson Academic Language List

1. Accompany
2. Acknowledge
3. Administrate
4. Advocate
5. Apparent
6. Aspect
7. Authentic
8. Behalf
9. Cherish
10. Commence
11. Compensate
12. Comprehensive
13. Conceive
14. Confer
15. Consent
16. Consist
17. Constitute
18. Contradict
19. Contradict
20. Converse
21. Crucial
22. Deconstruct
23. Deduce
24. Despite
25. Deviate
26. Discrepancy
27. Discriminate
28. Displace
29. Distinct
30. Enforce
31. Explicit
32. Fluctuate
33. Forecast
34. Format
35. Forthcoming
36. Generate
37. Guideline
38. Ideology
39. Ignorance
40. Implicit
41. Impose
42. Incidence
43. Incorporate
44. Index
45. Infrastructure
46. Inherent
47. Inherit
48. Initiate
49. Innovate
50. Integral
51. Intensity
52. Intervene
53. Isolate
54. Maximize
55. Minimize
56. Negate
57. Orient
58. Perceive
59. Perspective
60. Precede
61. Refine
62. Regulate
63. Resolve
64. Restrain
65. Reveal
66. Scrutinize
67. So-called
68. Somewhat
69. Specify
70. Sufficient
71. Supplement
72. Transmit
73. Undergo
74. Utilize
75. Violate

11th Grade Social Science (Bricks) Academic Vocabulary List

1. 9/11
2. Affirmative Action
3. American Revolution
4. Antebellum Period
5. Appeasement
6. Arms Race
7. Articles of Confederation
8. Berlin Wall
9. Bicameral
10. Bill of Rights
11. Blockade
12. Checks and Balances
13. Civil Rights
14. Civil War
15. Cold War
16. Colonist
17. Communism
18. Compromise of 1850
19. Confederate
20. Congress
21. Constitutional
22. Continental Congress
23. Counterculture
24. D-Day
25. Domestic
26. Domino Theory
27. Dust Bowl
28. Equal Rights
29. Espionage
30. Fascism
31. Federalism
32. Feminism
33. French & Indian War
34. Gold Rush
35. Great Awakening
36. Holocaust
37. International
38. Internment
39. Iraq War
40. Jamestown
41. Korean War
42. Louisiana Purchase
43. Loyalist
44. Manifest Destiny
45. Monopoly
46. NATO
47. New Deal
48. Oregon Trail
49. Pearl Harbor
50. Plymouth Rock
51. Populism
52. Preamble
53. Progressivism
54. Prohibition
55. Proliferation
56. Propaganda
57. Quotas
58. Revolutionary War
59. Secession
60. Segregation
61. Social Security
62. Socialism
63. Spanish American War
64. State's Rights
65. Supreme Court
66. Tariffs
67. Temperance
68. Totalitarianism
69. Transcendentalism
70. Trusts
71. Vietnam War
72. War of 1812
73. Watergate
74. Women's Suffrage
75. Yankee

11th Grade Statistics (Bricks) Academic Vocabulary List

1. Bayesian analysis
2. Bimodal
3. Binomial coefficients
4. Boxplot
5. Census
6. Central tendency
7. Chi
8. Cluster
9. Combinatorics
10. Conditional probability
11. Correlation coefficient
12. Cumulant
13. Deciles
14. Deviation
15. Discrete variable
16. Disjoint events
17. Error analysis
18. Expected value
19. Fibonacci
20. Fibonacci
21. Fixed precision
22. Frequency distribution
23. Gambling odds
24. Geometric mean
25. Gradient
26. Harmonic mean
27. High quartile
28. Impossible events
29. Interpolation
30. Interquartile range
31. Iteration
32. Joint probability
33. Kendall operator
34. Least-squares fit
35. Linear regression
36. Mean of a random variable
37. Momental skewness
38. Mu
39. Multivariate
40. Mutually exclusive
41. Negatively associated data
42. Nominal scale
43. Nonparametric
44. Outlier
45. Paired data
46. Parameter
47. Pascal's triangle
48. Permutation
49. Pi
50. Positive direction
51. Quartiles
52. Quintiles
53. Random sample
54. Ratio scale
55. Real limits
56. Regression equation
57. Relative frequency
58. Residual
59. Root mean square
60. Sample size
61. Scatterplot
62. Sigma notation
63. Standard deviation
64. Standardized distribution
65. Statistical indices
66. Stem and leaf plot
67. Strata
68. Sum rule of probability
69. Sure event
70. Theta
71. Time-series analysis
72. Variance
73. Variation coefficient
74. Weighted average
75. Z-score

11ᵗʰ Grade Science (Bricks) Academic Vocabulary List

1. Acoustic
2. Adherent
3. Alchemist
4. Alimentary
5. Amniocentesis
6. Ampere
7. Amplitude
8. Anode
9. Asthenosphere
10. Attenuation
11. Buoyancy
12. By-product
13. Carcinoma
14. Cathode
15. Cervical
16. Chloroplast
17. Cold-blooded
18. Conduction
19. Contagion
20. Converter
21. Cytoplasm
22. Dioxin
23. Electron Microscope
24. Emphysema
25. Epinephrine
26. Estuary
27. Eukaryote
28. Gamete
29. Gastrointestinal
30. Histology
31. Hydrolysis
32. Ionic
33. Kelvin
34. Lactic
35. Lipids
36. Metastasis
37. Morphology
38. Myocardial
39. Newtons
40. Opthalmology
41. Paleontologist
42. Potential Energy
43. Prokaryote
44. Propagation
45. Refraction
46. Relative Humidity
47. Renal
48. Sublimation
49. Transducer
50. Warm-blooded

11th Grade Language Arts (Bricks) Academic Vocabulary List

1. Alibi
2. Ambiguous
3. Augment
4. Brevity
5. Coherent
6. Characterization
7. Controlling Image
8. Cynical
9. Diction
10. Digress
11. Discursive
12. Drivel
13. Epigraph
14. Etymology
15. Eulogize
16. Euphony
17. Exemplify
18. Extemporaneous
19. Extrapolate
20. Fervor
21. Flippant
22. Idiosyncrasy
23. Impartial
24. Impromptu
25. Lucid
26. Morphology
27. Oral Interpretation
28. Paradigm
29. Peripheral
30. Plagiarism
31. Plausible
32. Postulate
33. Preamble
34. Precedent
35. Predicament
36. Proponent
37. Rebuttal
38. Redundant
39. Refute
40. Resonate
41. Retraction
42. Reversal
43. Rhetoric
44. Semantics
45. Shakespearean
46. Stereotype
47. Succinct
48. Tangent
49. Underscore
50. Venerate

Chapter Eighteen:

Twelfth Grade Academic Language & Academic Vocabulary

*"A capacity and taste for reading
gives access to whatever has already
been discovered by others."*
Abraham Lincoln

As students enter their senior year of high school they are looking forward to college and career. Students will be taking college entrance exams (ACT, SAT, etc.) and a variety of other tests that will determine their admission to further training and education. Students planning on college should study the vocabulary and associated concepts that will help them out on the university entrance exams. Those students who are planning on attending a trade school or starting a career should consider the professional language registers of their chosen profession. For example, my oldest daughter pursued training as a cosmetologist so that she could have a trade and better income as she attended college. Learning the professional language of cosmetology was an important part of getting a job and doing well in the job. At the same time she needed the general academic language and specific content academic vocabulary as she entered college. With the bricks and mortar language to build the conceptual knowledge students will succeed in their academic and professional pursuits. The language and vocabulary accumulated over the years of schooling makes a huge difference in the opportunities and doors that will open for students as they prepare for graduation and their future life.

12th Grade (Mortar) Johnson Academic Vocabulary List

1. Accessorize
2. Accommodate
3. Albeit
4. Ambiguous
5. Append
6. Appropriate
7. Arbitrary
8. Assimilate
9. Calibrate
10. Cohere
11. Coherent
12. Coincide
13. Compute
14. Conciliate
15. Concurrent
16. Connote
17. Conscience
18. Constitute
19. Construct
20. Contact
21. Contemporary
22. Controversy
23. Convene
24. Criticize
25. Denotation
26. Denote
27. Discrete
28. Dismantle
29. Dominate
30. Duration
31. Elicit
32. Empirical
33. Encounter
34. Entity
35. Ethic
36. Excerpt
37. Exclude
38. Extrapolate
39. Henceforth
40. Implication
41. Imply
42. Incentive
43. Incline
44. Inevitably
45. Inherent
46. Institute
47. Isolate
48. Kinesthetic
49. Linguistic
50. Liquidate
51. Meta-Analysis
52. Notwithstanding
53. Orientate
54. Paradigm
55. Phenomenon
56. Preliminary
57. Probable
58. Protocol
59. Pseudo
60. Ramification
61. Repertoire
62. Scene
63. Speculate
64. Supplement
65. Surmise
66. Syntax
67. Synthesize
68. Tabulate
69. Tactile
70. Tangent
71. Terminate
72. Transparent
73. Underlie
74. Virtual
75. Whereby

12th Grade Social Science (Bricks) Academic Vocabulary List

1. Accrued
2. Aggregate Demand
3. Aggregate Supply
4. Annuity
5. Appellate
6. Bankruptcy
7. Budget
8. Capitalism
9. Census
10. Civil Disobedience
11. Civil Service
12. Collateral
13. Commodities
14. Congress
15. Conservatism
16. Consumption
17. Corporation
18. De facto
19. Deficit
20. Diversification
21. Electoral College
22. Eminent Domain
23. Entitlement
24. Entrepreneur
25. Equity
26. Estate
27. Federal Reserve
28. Filibuster
29. Fiscal Policy
30. Foreclosure
31. Foreign Policy
32. Gerrymandering
33. Globalization
34. Gross Domestic Product
35. Habeas Corpus
36. Identity Theft
37. Impeachment
38. Incentives
39. Income
40. Inflation
41. Interest Group
42. Interest Rates
43. Judicial Review
44. Jurisdiction
45. Laissez Faire
46. Liberalism
47. Lobbying
48. Market Economy
49. Mercantilism
50. Mortgage
51. Oligopoly
52. Opportunity Cost
53. Ordinance
54. Patronage
55. Platform
56. Profit
57. Recession
58. Redistricting
59. Regulation
60. Reimbursement
61. Repossession
62. Revenue
63. Services
64. Socio-economic
65. Specialization
66. Subsidy
67. Suffrage
68. Supply Curve
69. Trade Balance
70. Unemployment
71. Unsecured Debt
72. Utilities
73. Welfare
74. Writ of Habeas Corpus
75. Zoning

12th Grade Mathematics (Bricks) Academic Vocabulary List

1. Absolute maximum
2. Absolute minimum
3. Acceleration
4. Alternating series
5. Annulus
6. Approx. by differentials
7. Area between curves
8. Asymptote
9. Bounded function
10. Cartesian
11. Centroid
12. Constant term
13. Continuous function
14. Convergent sequence
15. Critical value
16. Cusp
17. Decreasing function
18. Definite integral
19. Delta
20. Derivative
21. Differential
22. Discontinuity
23. Divergent series
24. Exponential growth
25. Extremum
26. Fixed
27. Harmonic progression
28. Helix
29. Implicit differentiation
30. Improper integral
31. Indeterminate expression
32. Infinite limit
33. Infinitesimal
34. Instantaneous velocity
35. Integral table
36. Integration methods
37. Interval of convergence
38. Iterative process
39. Jump discontinuity
40. Limit comparison test
41. Local behavior
42. Logarithmic differentiation
43. Mean value theorem
44. Mesh
45. Multivariate
46. Norm of partition
47. Oblate spheroid
48. Ordinary differential equation
49. Orthogonal
50. Parallel cross sections
51. Parametrize
52. Piecewise function
53. Positive series
54. Power series convergence
55. P-series
56. Quotient rule
57. Rationalizing substitutions
58. Related rates
59. Removable discontinuity
60. Riemann sum
61. Rolle's theorem
62. Root test
63. Scalar
64. Secant
65. Secant line
66. Second order critical point
67. Shell method
68. Sigma notation
69. Simple harmonic motion
70. Solid of revolution
71. Step discontinuity
72. Taylor polynomial
73. Torus
74. Vector calculus
75. Washer method

12th Grade Science (Bricks) Academic Vocabulary List

1. Acetic
2. Anaerobic
3. Antibiotic
4. Antiseptic
5. Autoimmune
6. Bandwidth
7. Barometer
8. Capacitator
9. Concentric
10. Congenital
11. Convection
12. Covalent Bond
13. Deoxyribonucleic
14. Dermis
15. Electrodynamometer
16. Endocrine
17. Hypothalamus
18. Incision
19. Incubation
20. Interferon
21. Isotope
22. Malignant
23. Melanoma
24. Neurotransmitter
25. Nomenclature

26.
27. Ozone
28. Phagocyte
29. Pharmacology
30. Phosphorous
31. Positron
32. Posterior
33. Predisposed
34. Prognosis
35. Puerperal
36. Rectification
37. Refraction
38. Resonance
39. Roentgen
40. Sarcoma
41. Synapse
42. Synchronization
43. Tensile
44. Thalamus
45. Thrombosis
46. Thyroid
47. Translucent
48. Valence
49. Viscosity
50. Zygote Plankton

12th Grade Language Arts (Bricks) Academic Vocabulary List

1. Aesthetic
2. Ambivalence
3. Anapest
4. Anecdote
5. Appease
6. Archetype
7. Cajole
8. Candid
9. Cogent
10. Cognition
11. Colloquial
12. Credibility
13. Dactyl
14. Denouement
15. Derogatory
16. Didactic
17. Elucidate
18. Epigram
19. Epistle
20. Espouse
21. Euphemism
22. Exegesis
23. Extol
24. Extraneous
25. Fallacious
26. Germane
27. Histrionic
28. Iconoclast
29. Incongruous
30. Juxtapose
31. Loquacious
32. Metacognition
33. Metonymy
34. Motif
35. Nebulous
36. Onus
37. Orthodox
38. Orthography
39. Paradox
40. Parallelism
41. Polemic
42. Pontificate
43. Pragmatic
44. Prosody
45. Pyrrhic
46. Quatrain
47. Recapitulate
48. Reticent
49. Sardonic
50. Veracity

References

Alliance for Excellent Education (2009). http://www.all4ed.org/files/National_wc.pdf

Bearne, E., Dombey, H., & Grainger, T. (2006). Classroom interactions in literacy. Columbus, OH: McGraw Hill

Britt, R. (2009) http://www.livescience.com/3211-14-percent-adults-read.html

Cain, K. & Oakhill, J. (2007) Children's comprehension problems in oral and written languages. New York: Guilford Press.

Carlisle, J. & Rice, M. (2002). Improving Reading Comprehension: Research-based principles and practices. York Press Inc.

Common Core Standards: http://www.corestandards.org/

Dickson, S., Simmons, D., & Kameenui, E. (1995). Text organization: Curricular and instructional iimmplications for diverse learners (Technical Report No. 18). Eugene, OR: National Center to Improve the Tools of Educators.

Dictionary.com: http://dictionary.reference.com/

Farrell, T. (2000). Reflective practice in action: 80 reflection breaks for teachers. Thousand Oaks, CA: Corwin Press.

Francis, D., Rivera, M., Lesaux, N., Keiffer, M., & Rivera, H. (2006). Practical guidelines for the education of English language learners: Research-based recommendations for instruction and academic interventions. Portsmouth, NH: RMC Research Corporation, Center on Instruction.

Girard, V., & Spycher, P. (2007) Aiming High: A countywide commitment to close the achievement gap for English Learners. http://www.scoe.org/docs/ah/AH_girard.pdf

Gersten, R., Baker, S., Shanahan, T., Linan-Thompson, S., Collins, P, & Scarcella, R. (2007). Effective literacy and English language instruction for English learners in the elementary grades: A practice guide. Washington, DC: IES-USDE

Hart, B. & Risley, T. (2003) The early catastrophe: The 30 million word gap by age 3. *American Educator, 22,* 4-9.

Hirsch, E. (2006) The case for bringing content into the language arts block and for a knowledge-rich curriculum core for all children. American Educator. 30(1), 8-17.

Hirsch, E. (2003, Spring) Reading comprehension requires knowledge of words and the world: Scientific insights into the fourth-grade reading slump and the nation's stagnant comprehension scores. American Educator. 27(1) 10-29.

Honig, B., Diamond, L. & Gutlohn, L. (2000). Teaching Reading: Sourcebook for kindergarten through eighth grade. Novato, CA: Arena Press.

Hoy, W. & Miskel, C. (2002) Theory and Research in Educational Administration. Information Age Publishing: Charlotte, NC

Johnson, E. & Karns, M. (2011) RTI Strategies that work in the K-2 classroom. Larchmont, NY: Eye on Education.

Johnson, E. (2009) Academic Language! Academic Literacy!: A Guide for K-12 Educators. Thousand Oaks, CA: Corwin Press.

Kamil, M., Pearson, D. Moje, E., & Afflerbach, P. (2010) Hanbook of Reading Research. New York, NY: Routledge.

Kinsella, K. (2007). Rigorous and accountable academic discussion with the rbook.

Kozol, J. (1995) Amazing Grace: The lives of children and the conscience of a nation. New York, NY: Harper Collins.

Langer, J. (2001). Beating the odds: Teaching middle and high school students to read and write well. American Educational Research Journal. 38(4), 837-880.

Lyon, R. (2001). Measuring Success: Using assessments and accountability to raise student achievement. Washington DC: Subcommittee on Education Reform Committee on Education and the Workforce U.S. House of Representatives.

Marzano, R., Pickering, D. & Pollock, J. (2001) Classroom Instruction that Works: Research-Based Strategies for increasing student achievement. Alexandria, VA: ASCD.

Orfield, G. Losen, D., Wald, J. & Swanson, C. (2004). Losing our Future: How minority youth are being left behind by the graduation rate crisis.

Moats, L. (2000) Speech to Print: Language essentials for teachers. Baltimore, MD: Brookes.

Pearson, P., Hiebert, E., & Kamil, M. (2007). Vocabulary assessment: What we know and what we need to learn. Reading Research Quarterly, 42, 282-296.

Scarcella, R. (2003). Academic English: A conceptual framework. Irvine CA: UC-LMRI.

Schleppegrell, M. (2004) The language of schooling: A functional linguistic perspective.

Snow, C. & Biancarosa, G. (2003). Adolescent Literacy and the Achievement Gap: What do we know and where do we go from here? New York, NY: Carnegie Corporation.

Stronge, J. (2007). Qualities of effective teachers (2nd Ed.). Alexandria, VA: ASCD.

Wolfram, W., Adger, C. & Christian, D. (1999) Dialects in schools and communities. Mahwah, NJ: Lawrence Erlbaum Associates.

Appendix A:

Academic Language K-2 Graphic Organizer

Johnson Model

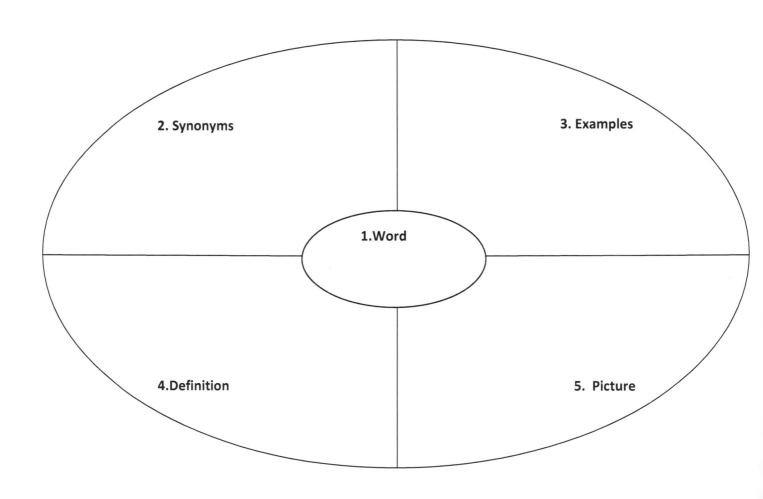

Appendix B:

Academic Language Graphic Organizer

Grades 3- 12 Johnson Model

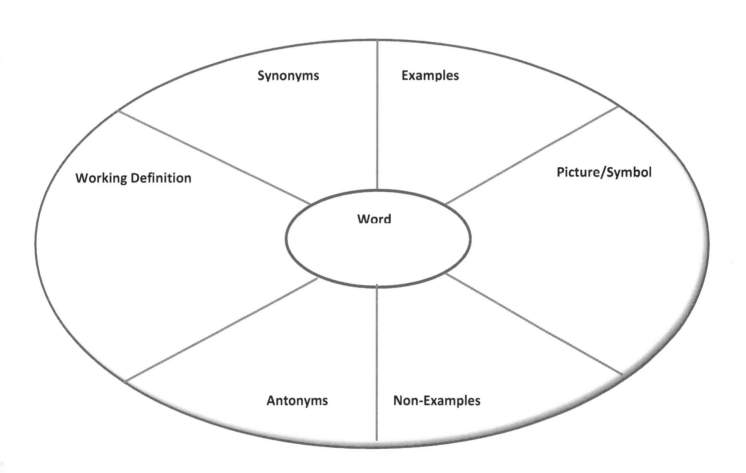

Made in the USA
Charleston, SC
18 June 2012